MW00973606

After the Rain,

the Sun Shines Brighter.

10 Steps to Greater Life Success

Revised edition

G. G. Bolich, Ph.D.

Psyche's

Press

Psyche's Press

Raleigh, NC

©2001, 2007 G. G. Bolich

Printed in the United States of America. All rights reserved. No part of this book may be used or reproduced in any manner whatsoever without permission, except in the matter of brief quotations employed in reviews or critical works. For permissions, please contact Dr. G. G. Bolich at ggbolich @earthlink.net.

ISBN 978-0-6151-5632-3

Dedication

This volume is affectionately dedicated to Susan, Chris and Ben, fellow travelers from storms to sunshine.

Table of Contents

Introduction.

Weathering the Storm

If I could, right now I would sit next to you in silence.

When you are thoroughly drenched by life's rains, wrenched with grief and bowed by defeat, words feel too little, too light, and too late. Only silence has the gravity right for such moments. So, if you will lend me your imagination, please see me sitting awhile beside you, holding my words while I keep faith with you in the solitude of shared misery. For it is true that misery loves company, but only the fellowship of shared silence where we know one another through our mutual experience of pain, loss and sorrow.

I am in no hurry. I will be here when you are ready for words.

What Can I Say to You?

Words are what I have to offer. Can they possibly be enough?

I don't know your pain, your loss, your defeat. How can I? Such things by their very nature slice our bonds to others, leaving us isolated and alone. No one can know your devastation in the manner you do.

But I can *imagine* it, just as you can imagine me sitting quietly beside you.

As you have done for others you care about, so I sit here in the silence and imagine what it must be like for you. I imagine how I would feel and speak and act if I were faced with what you are facing *right now*. In this manner I glimpse how hard it is to be where you are, to see what you see, and to face the day ahead. I open my mouth to speak, and pause. What can I say to you? How can I help?

An image comes to mind. I see us both beneath a sky as dark as death, roiling clouds heavy with oppressive rain. Our eyes meet briefly, only long enough to see how wet we are, and cold. A sharp wind howls and beats against us, sending biting drops to mix with our tears. We start toward one another but the ground gives way. We fall. Our eyes look toward each other again, and our mouths open. But the storm is too fierce for our words to overcome and we cannot best the elements to reach each other.

We are alone—and yet not. Though separate, we share the experience of the storm. We cannot speak directly—and yet we communicate. The storm breaks upon us—but we are not yet broken. Knowing you are there strengthens me; I hope knowing I am here does the same for you.

Though every storm is different, in many ways they are all alike. The skies grow dark, the wind rises, and rain comes. Caught outside we seek what shelter we can find, though we are likely drenched before we reach it. All thought of blue skies vanishes and the thunderous reality of the storm commands our every instinct for self-preservation. All we can cling to is a wish to survive, to outlast the fury.

I know you see my point. Life's storms mirror Nature's. And just as I can imagine us together in a storm outside, so I can imagine us together in other storms. I draw upon my own experiences of life's myriad storms to fuel my imagination, to lend credence to my thoughts and feelings, because these experiences can offer a bond between us, the shared cords of survivors.

Yet, if I were you I would want to offer challenge. In your place I would ask of me, "What have *you* survived that offers any credibility to being here? What do *you* know of pain, of loss, of defeat and suffering?"

The challenge is fair. You have every right to judge my credentials in the experience of life's storms as you would if I were applying for any other job. Truly, I am applying for a position with you as fellow traveler through the storm. You need to know if I can be trusted, if I have experience adequate to the task.

Perhaps a word or two on my own dark nights is in order.

A Curriculum Vitae

I cannot remember a time ever being free of pain, whether physical or emotional. I was a small, thin child, beset by the illnesses of childhood: mumps, both kinds of measles (and more than once), chickenpox, and so forth. To these I added the less common scourges, such as scarlet fever. But these were merely temporary veneers to more abiding problems. Born with skeletal defects, I wore casts to my hips when very young and had to learn to walk twice; I never owned a pair of regular shoes until I went to college. So near-sighted I was legally blind without glasses, my vision problems were not detected until I was ten years old. Plagued by allergies, I endured weekly shots and had a diet so limited that at one point all the foods I was permitted could be listed on a single sheet, with plenty of room to spare.

My curious gait, frequent skin rashes and occasional difficulties breathing, combined with poor eyesight, and the smallest, skinniest body in my class, made me the inevitable target of every bully I encountered throughout childhood. These same characteristics made me vulnerable to child abuse, despite the care and protection my parents tried to provide. It seemed whether at school or away, I was too often the object of ridicule, scorn, and physical aggression. I fought frequently—and always lost.

My efforts to defend myself were laughable—and often laughed at. My peers jeered at me, and most of my teachers seemed unsympathetic at best, callous at worst. I remember in sixth grade, after another lost fight, swinging my fists in frustration at the teacher who had intervened, laughing as he held me at arm's length. The following year, in more frustration at another teacher, I hit her over the head with a classroom chair. I was anxious and depressed, filled with longing for escape. In short, as a child I desperately wanted to reach what I thought would be the sanctuary of adulthood.

Being "grown up" did not turn out to be the refuge I had fantasized as a child. I spent most of college on probation—not for academic reasons, but because of altercations with faculty. I had learned early on not to expect authority figures like teachers or administrators to listen, and the lessons continued in my undergraduate years. So, too, did bodily trials. I had been made to give up baseball in high school because calcium deposits in my right elbow caused me to fail my physical. Treatment for this same condition as a college freshman produced a temporary paralysis that indicated a serious allergy to cortisone. Then, in my second year, I experienced a rare eye infection that induced the worst headache of my life, accompanied by light sensitivity so severe I spent ten weeks living in darkness.

Yet none of this compared to the pain I experienced from that all-too-common nemesis of youth: unrequited love. On my first summer break from college I experienced, quite literally, love at first sight. This was no mean feat, considering the object of my affection belonged to a set of identical twins. Three roller coaster years followed, ending finally in her irrevocable choice not to be with me.

All this, and I had barely arrived at adulthood.

A Case in Point

You and I both know the adult years have many challenges of their own. Storms paced my path as I married, had children, divorced, and went through a long dark night of the soul struggling in therapy to come to terms with my childhood and with my adult failings. At last I seemed to find a break among the clouds. I moved, took a new job, and began a new life with a supportive partner by my side.

But everything changes. The earth turns, the sun sets, darkness falls again. And in the night, more rain.

A life-altering storm broke upon me early on a Friday morning in May some years ago. I started the morning worried. I suspected my situation at work was not as secure as the leadership had reassured me. For consolation I had turned to a favorite book, the work of an ancient Roman philosopher who was an old friend in times when I needed to bolster my courage. While reading aloud to a friend some of the words of Seneca, a honking horn interrupted me. It was a messenger bearing bad news in the shape of a registered letter. The contents were brief, two short lines announcing that I was out of a job. I sat down with my friend, Ben, and tried to process the reality.

"This isn't fair. I don't deserve this," I said, stating the obvious. My mind flashed back to the night before, when the very individuals responsible for sealing my fate had participated in a public recognition of my work excellence, complete with a plaque and handshake. At the same time they were offering smiles and congratulations they knew my fate already had been sealed. I shook my head in a mix of shocked disbelief and complete disgust.

Ben at once reminded me of what I had been reading to him. I picked up the book and looked again at the words. "The fury of adversity cannot overcome the spirit of a steadfast man," the Roman philosopher had written. "It is not what, but how we endure that matters." What had been easy wisdom to agree to only moments before was now testing my mettle.

I sighed. In truth, my emotions were in turmoil. Part of me was greatly relieved. I had been under immense pressure as I tried to do the right thing in an environment that shared none of my values. On the other hand, I knew getting rid of me was meant to send a message to others who might take unpopular stands. Part of me wanted to fight back because what had happened was wrong. On the other hand, I was profoundly glad not to be working for people who could treat others like I had been treated.

But now I faced an important question: What do I do next?

Wet All Over

You may be asking the same question right now.

What storm is upon you? Have you recently experienced a broken relationship? Has your health taken a turn for the worse? Have you experienced a significant setback in your career? Are your drowning in loss and disappointment?

If you answered 'Yes' to any of the above, then you are probably looking for shelter. You may wonder if there is any cover from the downpour, any possibility of peace from the thunderous tumult. Right now it may seem so dark you can't help but worry that the sun will never shine again.

This book is intended for *you*. It doesn't matter if your storm was one visible from a long way off or suddenly appeared from a clear sky. Either way, in the resulting downpour of bad news and strong feelings you may be blinking back tears only to find you are wet all over. Worse, it may look like you will never be dry again.

I know the feelings. I know the questions. I am still damp from the downpour of outrageous misfortune. But I have survived. So will you. In fact, if you follow certain important steps, you may find that after the rain, the sun shines brighter. You can experience greater success than you have ever known.

Of course, you need to be clear what I mean by 'success.' This book isn't about managing your financial assets so as to make you a millionaire. Nor is it about building career skills to get you that coveted promotion. As far as I am concerned, material prosperity and career advancement have value only insofar as they contribute to your own overall health and well-being, and that of those you love. The steps set forth here won't hinder your quest for material prosperity and probably will help it—but that isn't their end.

Success occurs when you undertake a venture and achieve a result better than what you anticipated or had possessed before. Success often comes after an experiment; you devise something different, try it, and find a prosperous outcome. Success follows desire. You know what isn't working. You know what losses you have suffered. You know what you want, even if you do not believe you can have it. Success can only come if you acknowledge what you have lost, confess what you want, and take new chances.

Let's agree to be completely candid. We both know taking chances is hardest when things aren't going well. I am not asking you to accompany me down an easy path. But it is one that you *can* walk and that you do not have to walk alone. I won't make outrageous claims or promises; you have to be honest with yourself. Together we can get you moving again and you can bounce back with a reasonable hope of finding new and wondrous success.

The ten steps I am presenting matter. They do not guarantee your every fantasy will be fulfilled. These steps cannot stop life's storms—nothing can— but they can guide you to weathering the storm so that you come out the other side in a surprising fashion. These practical steps offer you a way to get back up in the middle of the rain and start walking through the storm toward the rainbow and sunshine on the other side.

Face it. Life brings *many* storms. Some are brief squalls, momentary interruptions in our journey. We plow through them, teeth gritted, and quickly forget them once they are behind us. Other storms are more enduring. Like a massive front that seems to make camp right at our doorstep, these storms soak us in a chilling tide of grief. Day after day the rain comes until we wonder if we ever knew anything else.

In my situation, the sudden loss of my job seemed to initiate many months of troubling experiences. As a college teacher, it was the wrong time of year to find a full time appointment for the upcoming academic year. Even part time positions were already filled. And I questioned whether I even wanted to remain in a profession increasingly subject to outside pressures, disrespect, and low rewards. After more than a quarter century in higher education, I wondered if it was time to explore new avenues. What was I to do?

Even as I struggled to answer that question, the economy decided to keep me company on my downward spiral. Many people became unwilling members of the long lines at the unemployment office. The country experienced several months of double-digit unemployment. My degrees and years of experience teaching made little impression on company managers faced with cutting personnel rather than adding and training people like me. I felt obsolete and unwanted.

I was middle-aged and emotionally unprepared for what I was experiencing. I had never lost a job before; everything I faced now was unexplored territory. Nor was I given the luxury of time to reflect on my new situation and plan carefully. I was immediately pressed by family turmoil, fiscal woes, and the ongoing hassles of daily life. In short, I was thoroughly soaked by this storm—wet all over.

In the midst of the thunder and lightning of life's chaos, I found more and more of my time consumed by one taunting, unanswerable query: *Why me?*

The Rain Falls on the Just and Unjust Alike

The question seems inevitable. Though hardly perfect, I am a good person. I did not deserve to lose my job. In fact, I was sure the experience would have been easier to bear had I been able to find some fault in my performance. But there was nothing to find—no complaints, no reprimands, no warnings. And when it happened, no explanation. It truly wasn't fair, and being denied any due process appeal underscored that unfairness.

I already knew life isn't fair; we all know that. But head knowledge was vigorously contesting with my gut, which kept screaming that such things ought not to happen. The very value system that made me a target at work now rose to afflict me at home. Ironically, as a teacher of psychology I had often told others that life beats up on us enough we need not beat up on ourselves. Yet I had trouble letting go of my pain. Like an impatient child, I kept scratching at the scab, reopening the wound.

I tried to console myself. 'The rain falls on the just and unjust alike,' I would remind myself. But always came the rejoinder, 'Yeah, but the just sure get wetter.' At least, so it seemed to me. I became morose. As my despondency grew, my energy flagged. It grew harder and harder to drag myself out of bed and make any effort. Why bother? No one wanted me. I was through, washed up, a has-been before fifty.

Singing in the Rain

Yet life moves inexorably on.

Slowly—way too slowly—I began to see that as long as I was going to have to slog through puddles I could either do it with my head down, staring at the mud, or with my eyes raised, waiting for the clouds to part. I could march to a funeral dirge or lift my heels and sing in the rain. I won't pretend I distinguished myself in song, nor will I claim that once I decided to lift my head I never lowered it again. I had a few good days and many more bad ones. I slipped and slid, started and sputtered more times than I can count. In fact, the final line in my story isn't written yet. I still have crises of confidence and fall back into the depressing mud.

Yet I keep on getting up again.

Actually, with rain in my face all the time it is easy to wash away the mud. I see some things more clearly than ever. I have been paying attention in this school of hard knocks. Amidst the thundering roar there have been illuminating flashes. The storm has taught me some worthwhile lessons.

Nor am I above learning from the misfortunes of others. Contrary to our feelings of isolation when our eyes are darkened by rough times, we are not alone. In fact, others lost in storms of their own surround us. But they are not the only ones. Many enjoying brighter times see our rough weather and offer shelter, support, and experience from former storms. I learned to look anew at those around me, both others under duress and those survivors who offered their help to me. They taught me much through their stories.

I want to share these lessons with you even though I know you will learn most things the same way we all do—by riding the whirlwind. That's okay. Getting battered by the storm helps turn head knowledge into felt experience. It breeds wisdom. In the long run, getting wet all over offers us a chance to cleanse ourselves.

Right now you may have strong doubts about that claim. So did I. Not one of these lessons came easy to me. Every step was a struggle. Maybe that's why they matter so much to me now.

If you can accept that your storm's rain is falling on the fertile field of a receptive soul, then you can commit your hands to the work of building greater success than you have ever known. I will be with you every step along the way. I'm used to being wet. Together we can find the sun again. In that spirit—and for that success—this book is written.

But know this: ultimately, this is a *self* help book. I can't do the work for you. No one else can. The sad truth about self-help books is that more of them are sold than are read, and more are read than actually used. This book won't help you sitting on a shelf, and just reading it won't get you where you want to go. I am doing my part. Please do yours.

Here is what I recommend. Try to use this 10 step plan as a course of action over the next 10 weeks. You will find each step leads to the next, but is complete in itself. Don't get hung up on what may seem like gimmicks—if you think that way you'll sabotage yourself by justifying not doing something because it seems too artificial. Have faith in the process.

You'll soon see, if you haven't already, that I use a lot of alphabetical lists and short phrases. These are a great example of what might look like a gimmick. So what? They are meant to aid memory, which is meant to help you with that week's plan. The bottom line for each of us is this: will we use what we are offered to help ourselves, or will we find an excuse not to do what we know needs to be done? Just do the work!

Right now we are meeting in the mud and muck. I have my hand out. Maybe it looks like all that's up my rain-soaked sleeve is a bunch of questionable tricks. But the hand is out. What have you got to lose?

Step 1.

Affirm Yourself

The road to brighter sunshine starts beneath dark clouds.

If you and I are to reach that sunshine, let us at least be honest about where we met. Here we are, in the middle of the storm. It's awful. Bad weather, especially when it lingers, is disheartening. And just when we need optimism and spirit the most, both are hardest to find. We grow pessimistic and depressed. Life's storm undermines our sense of self-confidence—and sometimes our very sense of self.

If you lose your sense of self, all is lost. So our first challenge is to find a way for you to keep yourself intact. We cannot let the storm shake you apart. I can tell you, 'Affirm yourself!'—it may sound like a perfectly splendid thing to do—but we both know it isn't as easy as it sounds. Yet it can be done.

My friend Carol's sense of self was sharply challenged when she lost her husband Bob. He had been, in her own words, 'my very reason for being.' When he died suddenly in an automobile accident, she lost more than her life partner; she momentarily lost her sense of who she was. An awful storm engulfed her. In her grief she felt wrenched apart, her husband's death leaving her nothing but tattered shreds and gaping emptiness.

When we talked soon after the tragedy, she spoke in fragments, her eyes downcast, her hands moving restlessly from her hair to her clothes, to each other. There were no children, and relations with family were distant. Carol felt absolutely bereft and terribly alone. Nor was I about to tell her how she should feel. I have known enough loss of my own to understand that no words can fill the void. Whatever she felt, she felt—and it was okay.

But Carol was *not* alone. That perfectly natural sense was factually incorrect. She and Bob had built a rich network of friends. They were truly both his friends and hers. Moreover, despite having built her life around Bob, I knew Carol had rich reserves she could now call upon. I had known Carol much longer than Bob had, and I remembered the strong, independent woman she had been. Although she had made Bob the center of her life, she had not lost those qualities that had allowed her to live by herself.

Understandably, her grief kept her blind to those things for a time. But as surely as day follows night, the brightness of her vitality slowly emerged again. We, her friends, were there for her to share her grief. We were also there to cheer her on as she rebuilt her life. We did not patch her together again; none of us can do that for one another. What we did do was listen and encourage her voice. Through her own voice Carol spoke her way back to wholeness.

How did she do this? How can *you* do it?

Let's be practical. It didn't happen instantly for Carol, nor did it for me—and it won't for you. Building the self is like building a house. If you want to build a house, you start with the foundation. Unless it is sound, you build in vain. The house of your own life, like Carol's, may seem shaken to the very foundation about now. So an inspection is in order. Whether you choose to repair the foundation you have already laid, or build anew, the goal is the same: a sound foundation.

Keep that image firmly in mind. Carol found it an especially appropriate metaphor because she and Bob had been planning that very task when he died. They had spent months drawing up plans for their dream home. The terminology of house building was fresh in her mind and she used it as she talked herself back to wholeness. She described her life as a house razed to the ground by fire. But she was determined to start amid the ashes and build anew.

Like Carol, you and I are going to establish four square corners to get your foundation properly aligned. We are going to call the foundation 'Self' and each corner is going to help ensure realizing your goal of becoming the person you want and need to be for greater success. Carol had to do this work because the storm not merely challenged her; it changed her. My own storm was different, but it also challenged and changed me. The nature of life's turbulence is to stir things up. We may be left with ruins, yet the stuff is always there from which rebuilding can begin.

Just to be clear with you, the four corners to this foundation of the self are:

- Accepting yourself.
- Believing in yourself.
- Caring for yourself.
- Depending on yourself.

These make a nice little ABCD alphabet you can very easily remember.

Are you ready to start? All it requires, right now, is your desire. You don't even have to believe—just *want* it.

Accept Yourself

I am here to tell you that there is hope. You are the source of that hope. If you have invited me into your storm, then I know something important: you are ready to get on with your life and attain to greater success than ever before. Your readiness tells me that inside you want to succeed and deep down you believe you can. In short, you have already told me enough for me to know you have reason to hope.

What you may be lacking is an awareness of this truth about yourself.

Carol really believed her life was over when Bob died. For her the first glimmer of light in the blackness came from a remark made by one of her friends. "What are you going to do about the house?" She told me that one question recalled her to a sense of purpose. Bob had died, but their business together was not finished. She still had things to do for both of them. In that realization she regained a bit of herself.

Carol reframed the question to herself: "What am *I* going to do about the house?" She realized this was now all about herself. She had to make the decisions about the house project—and about herself. Where was she headed? Who would she be now? Did she have what it took to manage on her own? The idea of the house focused her. In asking, and beginning to answer the questions, she was finding her own voice again.

I am a little slower on the uptake than Carol. In my storm I found that questions battered me rather than focused me. Where Carol began to find her voice in the storm, I found my own voice deafening. I was adding to the sound and fury around me. In short, unlike Carol, I was engaged in self-talk that was tearing me further apart.

Who are you more like—Carol, or me? Do you readily see all you still have left in the middle of all you have lost? What are you saying about yourself? Can you even hear your own voice above the roar of the storm?

In the middle of the crashing thunder you may find it hard to hear your voice affirming any good qualities that you can build upon. You and I need to tune in to your voice, strengthen it, and build its vocabulary. In fact, as you have glimpsed, the four corners we are laying for your foundation form an alphabet of the language you can use to build yourself up for the labor ahead.

I like using little language games to help make things easier. In tough times, as stress mounts, I find my mind slows, my memory holds less, and I don't focus as well. I need to keep things simple and to make them clear. Although they are certainly gimmicks, using certain language games helps me—and that's all that matters to me. If they seem somehow silly to others, so what? Those in sunshine don't need extra light. But when I am under heavy darkness, I'll take help wherever I can find it.

I also know that we tend to feel like we think, and we tend to think like we talk. So anything we can do to make our self-talk better may aid our thinking and help us feel better. So I use my gimmicks to help me talk more rationally to myself. I use them to bring me focus. I let them help me.

So let us start with the self-talk you are using right now. Listen to yourself. What kinds of things are you saying to yourself as the rain soaks you? I wager some of those things—maybe most—aren't very positive. That's okay—it is perfectly normal to be a bit gloomy when soaking wet. Before anything can change we have to be honest about where we are. So just listen carefully and hear what you are saying to yourself.

I found myself echoing the words of a family member, who in an angry outburst said, "You are such a loser! You can't even hold on to a job!" The tiny voice that protested that wasn't true got lost in the wave of guilt and doubt and loss that crashed that message down on me. I couldn't get it out of my head. Every new rejection—and there were plenty!—only made the message louder. Soon I was extending it to matters beyond employment. Every disagreement with someone meant I was a loser at relationships. Each time I experienced difficulty in a task I felt as though I might as well quit because I was 'a loser.'

Not only was that self-talk unhelpful, it was plain wrong. I am not a loser and neither are you. But I felt like one and I was in serious danger of acting like one because my thinking was distorted. The words I was saying to myself were wrong and hurtful. I needed to challenge them. I needed to learn a new language to speak truthful and uplifting words to myself.

After all, if my incorrect thinking was leading my feelings astray and jeopardizing the things I tried to do, then maybe correcting my thinking could help me feel better and perform better. It was worth a shot. No matter how strong my feelings were, I had to challenge them with things I knew were facts. Solid evidence existed that I had not always failed. How could I be a loser is I didn't always lose? In fact, over the course of my life, I had succeeded a fair number of times at various things. Just because I didn't feel like a winner at the moment didn't make those facts go away. I was just ignoring them. That had to change.

What message are you giving yourself? Before we recover the facts you are ignoring, let's first get at the message you are sending to yourself. Grab a piece of scrap paper (or use the space below), and write it down *right now*. I'll wait.

Seriously, I'll wait. I know how easy it is to say things like, 'I don't need to write it down. I know what I say,' or 'I will do it later.' You can fudge if you want, and just keep reading, but if you are serious about laying the cornerstone right, then take the time and make the effort. *Do it now.* If you need more space, here it is!

Good for you. If you are faithful in little things, I know you will be faithful in the larger ones. Now look back over what you have written. I hope there are some positive things there, but it is okay if there are not. After all, you are wet all over. It may be hard to see or say much nice or to be cheery. Right now all that matters is that you got the message out in the open. By objectifying it, the message becomes separate from you in a way that lets you see and hear it differently. That gives you a chance to change it.

Remember Carol? The first time she sat down to look at the house plans she and Bob had been working on all she could do was weep. Although the task initially had given her a point of focus, the work itself still felt too big. She had started talking positively to herself, but her self was being built bit-by-bit and it wasn't very far along yet. She was still too conscious of the rain to be able to see past the clouds to the sun she wanted to believe could be out there. She struggled over her need to do the very thing she found too hard to accomplish. She sensed that the real battle was for herself, not just getting a house built.

Carol needed to back up a little to firmer ground. She dried her eyes and reviewed the questions she had been asking herself. Where I heard the criticisms of others—and added my own—Carol heard only questions. But they refocused her and she took her time answering them. She let them tumble out, looked at them, and then set about making an orderly list. It might not have looked like much, but it was an important step.

Perhaps what you wrote down were questions. Maybe your message to yourself right now is one large question mark. That is okay too. Journeys begin by asking where one is and where one wants to go. Questions can be very positive because they can focus our attention and direct it. In that way we can begin sorting out things and reestablishing order in life. If you experience the questions as negative because you don't want to face them or can't see any answers, then it is good to be honest about it. Either way, if you wrote questions down, good for you! As with statements, writing the questions down objectifies them. They are now sitting there waiting for you. You are in control.

Now take a nice clean sheet of paper. I recommend using a nice piece of stationery or résumé paper. For this activity you deserve the best paper. Looking at the negative statements or questions you wrote on the scrap paper, intentionally challenge each one by writing an affirmation on your new piece of paper. Don't worry if the affirmation feels dishonest; your feelings aren't facts and we are interested in facts. So make sure what you write is factually correct.

For example, consider how each of these statements I used to say about myself were altered to more accurate statements:

- *Accusation*: "You are such a loser! You can't even hold on to a job." *Reply*: "I did lose my job. But I can't be a loser because I have held other jobs and succeeded at many things."

- *Accusation*: "You can't do anything right!" *Reply*: "Well, I can't do everything perfectly—but no one can. Even though I often overlook it, I do many things well."

- *Accusation*: "This time you really blew it. You'll never get another chance!" *Reply*: "Another chance at what? Screwing up? I doubt that! I'm sure I'll have many more chances to blow it, which means an equal number of chances to get it right!"

- *Accusation*: "You haven't got what it takes to succeed." *Reply*: "Who knows? All I need is what it takes to try. No one can guarantee success anyway. But I can guarantee I will try my best."

You aren't perfect. So what? Who is? But you aren't so flawed that you can say, 'Abandon hope all ye who enter!' Find the truth and write it down. Then enjoy yourself destroying that scrap paper. Put the realistic message where it is in easy reach. Use it when you need it.

Self-acceptance, the cornerstone of the foundation of Self, is essential to success. It means being honest with yourself. Perhaps you brought the rain upon yourself. Maybe you deserve to be wet. If so, own up to it. Just avoid the erroneous conclusion that the past dictates the future. Just as you made the bed you are now lying in, you can get up, make it over, and move on.

Start practicing a self-talk characterized by what I call 'kind truths.' These are messages rooted in fact but couched in gentle terms. If the fact is you messed up, then say 'I messed up; wasn't the first time and won't be the last. But I can do better; I have done better and I will do better!' Find ways to affirm yourself as you accept yourself.

Believe in Yourself

The next corner to help establish your foundation is self-belief. Unless you can believe you have the ability to move forward and attain more than you ever have, you will undermine your efforts. Of course, this corner depends on the cornerstone having been laid properly. You won't believe in yourself if you cannot accept who you are. Fortunately, believing in yourself does not require viewing yourself as perfect. All it requires is an act of will to accept that the resources you possess are sufficient to move you forward.

Remember how I said that laying a foundation for the Self involves some self-assessment? You began that with the cornerstone as you examined your negative self-talk and decided to challenge it with more realistic kind truths. Now it is time to go further. You need to establish an accurate basis for your belief in yourself. It is time to add some more kind truths to your new language of self-talk.

I hope you have some more nice paper at hand. Take another sheet and list reasons why your belief in yourself is well founded. I'll illustrate with my own list of 'Ten Reasons to Believe':

- I am a survivor. Somehow, I managed to get to this point alive so I must be doing some things right!

- I have good instincts. At this very time when things are tough and I have some self-doubt, I am doing some very right things, like reaching out for help.

- I am honest. Instead of playing games with myself, I have looked myself square in the mirror, owned up to who I am right now, and accepted myself.

- I am brave. Many people would not handle what I am going through as well as I am. Many people cannot find the courage to face themselves or life. I am doing both. I have the guts needed to do hard things.

- I am smart. Certainly I am smart enough to know that the occasional mistaken idea or dumb move does not make me an idiot—it makes me human. I know I can figure out ways to weather this storm and return to the sunshine.

- I am capable. In fact, it is almost scary how well I am actually doing considering how wet I am. Despite everything, I am still here, still functioning, and still managing many things well.

- I am decent. I haven't let this storm wear away my values, my sense of fair play, or my desire to be a good person. I still treat others like I want to be treated. No matter how much I hurt, I don't willingly hurt others. I am a good person.

- I am determined. Sure, I sometimes feel like giving up, but I haven't. I keep on doing things to make a difference. I will keep trying as hard as I can.

- I am creative. Amazingly, this storm has brought out some unexpected creativity as I have scrambled to find ways to cope. I never knew how creative I could be—and I don't want to give it up now.

- I am insightful. After all, I just proved I know myself well enough to establish ten reasons to believe in myself! That quality will stand me in good stead as I build toward greater success.

Perhaps you and I share some common reasons for self-belief. For instance, you have already shown your courage in picking up this book and reading this far. Trust me, as someone who has worked with people for more than a quarter century, I know how much courage it takes to break your isolation and reach out to potential helpers. Good for you!

When self-doubt assails you, return to your list. You have reasons to believe in yourself. Don't lose sight of them.

Care for Yourself

The third corner can be the hardest one to measure and place. You have been hurt and experienced loss. Pretending that isn't true is as self-destructive as the opposite extreme of wallowing in the wound, believing it is fatal. You must bind up your wound, give yourself time to heal, and recover your strength.

As hard as it may be to accept and believe in yourself, it may be harder to care for yourself. I went through a long period where I was so depressed I stopped taking care of myself. I ate little, slept little, and felt miserable. I struggled on the one hand with feeling like I didn't deserve to be cared for, and on the other hand with feeling like it wouldn't make any difference anyway. Maybe you have had similar feelings.

However, your first two corners have given you a basis for justifying self-care. Besides, I know you want to feel better. If you aren't caring for yourself it is because you are punishing yourself. That has to stop. Your sentence has been served. It is time to re-enter the land of the free.

Good things follow from self-care. Continuing care for yourself builds your self-respect. That effort in turn encourages respect from others. Time really does heal wounds, and working tenderly to assist time shows both your hope for the future and your willingness to live. Self-care is a precious gift.

Caring properly for yourself, though, requires an ongoing effort. Each day you must eat properly, get enough sleep, find time to exercise, and tend to your emotional equilibrium. For the latter, set aside a definite and limited time (perhaps a half hour) to think about and handle your emotional distress. During the rest of the day, as you busy yourself with productive tasks, refer your thoughts and feelings about your hurt to that time which you have set aside to deal with them. In this manner you can keep your focus and move forward.

Depend on Yourself

I think I am dependable, and I appreciate your trust in inviting me in to share your journey through the storm. But if you are going to depend on me, please only do it like one team member depends on another. We each have our role to play. You can depend on me to do my job, but you still have to do yours. In fact, I'm depending on you!

My role is like that of a hired guide. I have been through the storm and know there is sunshine on the other side. You may have doubts about that, but you have hired me on because you hope I'm right. My job is to point the way. Your job is to walk the path. We won't get out of the rain unless you do your part too.

You may not feel up to the task. When I was in my storm there were days I wanted to just lay in the puddles. Maybe it was my longing to be warm and dry that got me up each time, but I did it—and so can you. Despite what you may think, you have everything you need immediately at hand to get up out of the mud and start moving through the rain. You can't dodge the drops, but you can get out of the deep puddles and seek higher ground.

This corner can be the easiest to place because all you need do is line it up with the others. The hard corners have been set. Depending on yourself now is a rational and welcome task. You know you have the resources and you know you want to do it. Now it is an act of will.

You are ready to depend on yourself. You have taken the first step. In carefully aligning four square corners, you have made possible a foundation to build a structure straight and true. The four corners form an alphabet to build a language around: acceptance, belief, care, and dependence on yourself.

Now you are ready to build on these ABCs.

Writing Space

Please use this space for notes to yourself as you work through chapters 1-2.

Step 2.

Build on What You Have

Congratulations. You now have taken a first step to greater success. You have set out four corners straight and true for a sound foundation of the Self. Now you are ready to build. You are on your way out of the rain and into the sun of a brighter Self and future.

Building a house, a journey, or a life necessitates a plan. Having affirmed yourself, it is time now to plan what you want your Self and your journey to become. This merits the very best effort you can muster. We are going to plan like a pro, using professional kinds of strategy. The resources and tools you will use are what you have at hand right now. You have everything you need to get started.

Once more, we are going to use a simple language game of building an alphabet to keep us on track. Our ABCs this time around all have to do with careful planning. Although there can be many steps to creating an effective plan, we are going to start with four basic strategic elements. These will help you form a framework for further work.

Asset Assessment

A builder must first know what *assets* are at hand. Right now, you may have doubts about how many or how good your assets are. Keep affirming yourself because it is imperative you see clearly the real assets you possess. I am referring first to those qualities you have that brought you success in the past. In fact, take a moment to list them so you have a starting-point. You will find these assets fit on some of the other lists you will be making.

Let's start with assessing your *personal* assets. These are characteristics of body, mind, and spirit. You will again need a nice clean sheet of quality paper (or you can use the space provided below). Divide it into three columns, like so:

<u>Body</u>   <u>Mind</u>   <u>Spirit</u>

Under each column list at least seven personal qualities that can reasonably be viewed as positive. It is okay if some of the assets you list are taken from the work you did in the first step. However, challenge yourself to come up with at least seven additional qualities. You want to be factual and you want to practice speaking kind truths to yourself. This is not the time to put yourself down or depreciate what you have to offer. These are *assets*—possessions of value. Here is space for *your* list:

Body	Mind	Spirit
1.		
2.		
3.		
4.		
5.		
6.		
7.		

Perhaps you and I will share some common assets. My lists for each column look like this:

Body	Mind	Spirit
Able	Creative	Open
Intact	Flexible	Searching
Coordinated	Analytical	Intuitive
Fit	Methodical	Sensitive
Good hands	Disciplined	Passionate
Strong enough	Good memory	Caring
Dependable	Likes to think	Restless

These are kind truths. For instance, my body, while not perfect, is generally able and dependable. My mind does pretty well at breaking things down—a useful skill in an academic realm. My spirit is sensitive, meaning I can be easily hurt, but also meaning I can feel other's pain in ways I've learned to sometimes make useful to them. Your words will have special connotations for you as mine do for me.

Perhaps some of my assets surprised you. For example, "restless" may not seem to you like a positive quality of spirit. However, despite its downside, for me this is an asset. My restless spirit helps keep me open and searching; together those three spiritual assets encourage me that I am engaged in a meaningful life quest. I am a pilgrim on a journey whose end is not in sight.

Next let's consider your *relational* assets. These are the relationships you can count on. They include those who you know are sympathetic or supportive. They include your allies. Once more you will be using three columns. This time their headings are:

Family   Friends   Other Allies

The first two columns are self-evident. The third column is for the living connections we forge with nonhumans. Your pets, for example, are assets. They remain loyal to you, trusting and faithful, through thick and thin. Their love is an asset you can draw upon. If you have a relationship with some power greater than yourself, that also is an important asset. Through that relationship you may experience strength, support, hope, and love to sustain you in the darkness and move you toward the light.

Sometimes we have assets right under our nose that we take so for granted we forget they are there. Often we do that with family and friends. Take a moment to name those who have strong connections with you and who are on your side. Though they cannot experience the storm exactly like you do, they are wet too. But they *choose* to be wet in order to stay by your side. I cannot imagine stronger assets to draw upon as you build. Here's space for your list:

Family   Friends   Other Allies

1.

2.

3.

4.

5.

6.

7.

Next, let's evaluate your *contextual* assets. These are the resources available through your actual present situation. They include all of the following:

1. your age;
2. your education, training, and experience;
3. your geographical location;
4. the available market (e.g., for jobs or for relationships); and,
5. your culture and/or subcultures.

Make a list that takes into account each of the above contextual features. In a short sentence or two describe how each is an asset to you. For example, your age may be an asset because of the experience you have acquired (if older), or because of your energy and flexibility (if younger). You may belong to a specific cultural group that offers a distinctive sense of identity and connection. Try to see the value provided by these contextual factors. Here is space for your work:

1. Age: _____

2. Education:

   Training:

   Experience:

3. Geographical location:

4. Available market:

5. Culture/Subculture

If you honestly don't see something as an asset, then use that insight to contemplate a constructive change. For instance, I was once at a point where my geographical location seemed to me a strong negative. I moved and it was a life-affirming change that still carries benefits.

Finally, let's review your *material* assets. While I regard these as the least consequential, they certainly are not inconsequential. These assets include the following:

1. your finances;

2. your residence; and,

3. your belongings.

Don't worry too much right now if you lack some things or have less than what you'd like. The fact is, whatever you have is an asset, since nothing is owed you in life! Here is space to write:

1. Finances:

2. Residence:

3. Belongings:

Generally, material things are a mixed blessing. The many belongings you surround yourself with can also trap you. The goal in asset assessment is to see what ways these material things provide value you can use. For instance, your finances right now may be unstable or otherwise not what you would like. Is there anyway that apparent negative can be seen as having a silver lining? In the midst of poverty I remind myself how wonderful it is I have so little to lose! I also enjoy window-shopping and I know that the toys I might desire will be as enjoyable to me tomorrow—when I can afford them—as they would be today. In short, I choose to see the ways in which my actual material condition provides assets.

I urge you to learn asset assessment very well. Although it is especially important after a setback, it is never unimportant. Periodic asset assessment is valuable, too. The process keeps you in touch with your developing personal portfolio. It allows you another way to track your progress and provides more factual data you can use in affirming yourself. Finally, it helps keep you in tune with your goals. As your assets develop they may fine tune your journey, clarify your dreams, or point you in new directions.

Buy Low, Sell High

Our second element seems so obvious you may wonder why I bring it up and what it means for you. The logic is simple: to turn a profit we must make or purchase materials or services for less than what we sell them for. You are in need of selling yourself. This is true whether your need is to bounce back from deep depression, a lost love, or a career setback. In every case, you must find new ways to market yourself.

I realize this way of talking may seem dehumanizing. I am asking you to regard yourself as a commodity. I don't for a moment think of you as a product, but I am realistic enough to know that many people regard others that way. They want only to know what someone has to offer as a product or as a provider of services. I may not like it, but that doesn't excuse me from having to develop an ability to think this way to advance my own goals.

To sell yourself, start with what you have. You have completed an asset assessment so you know some of what you have to offer. Each one of these assets potentially can be enhanced or developed. Collectively they can be arranged in the most appealing manner possible to convey a genuine impression that also offers you the maximum favorable exposure.

This philosophy depends on being sold on yourself. Once more you need to see how essential self-affirmation is. If you can't sell yourself to yourself, then who else will be convinced? On the other hand, if you really are sold on yourself, and that sale has come from a realistic asset assessment, then you should do well selling yourself to others.

Let's see what your selling skills look like. Take a fresh sheet of paper and imagine you are purchasing space for an advertisement. Write an ad selling yourself. Limit yourself to twenty-five words or less. Here's mine:

> *For sale*: honest, personable, dependable individual who enjoys solitary pursuits but is able to work well with others. Competitive prices.

Here is space for yours:

Now that you have constructed an ad, look at it carefully. See what you have chosen to emphasize. These are assets you have arranged. Did you put them in an order to highlight your best features? Do they really say about you what you want them to say? Do they represent something different from what you have used in the past? This last point is especially important if your past efforts have not garnered for you what you want. If what you have been doing hasn't worked—try something different!

You can do this same exercise with advertisements of various lengths. The practice will be good and the insights you gather can be helpful to your planning and marketing alike.

Cost-Benefit Analysis

Every choice comes at a cost—*every* choice. You best be aware, honest, and committed to weighing the benefit you can gain against its price. Cost-benefit analysis has several values:

1. it develops an effective, purposeful approach to decision-making;

2. it helps curb impulsiveness by checking a one-sided emphasis on the benefit; and,

3. it also helps control undue caution by checking a one-sided emphasis on the cost.

Used properly, this can be a valuable part of planning and building.

Cost-benefit analysis is a process that leads to a product. As a process, it takes time and depends on information. The product can only be as good as the information it uses and the care with which that is weighed. To maximize cost-benefit analysis you need to be aware of several things.

1. The purpose is utilitarian; that is, it aims at being a useful tool. It does not provide guarantees of success.

2. The analysis works in probabilities. It only can say, 'based on this information, this is more likely than that.' That goes for both the costs and the benefits.

3. The calculation includes both the magnitude of the expected benefit (its value to you), and the likelihood of gaining it (an aspect of cost), as well as the effort involved (another part of the price).

4. The process emphasizes tradeoffs. It accepts that something is given up to gain something else. If you aren't willing to give anything up (i.e., pay the price), then you won't acquire the benefits.

You would do well to also reflect on the kind of buyer you are. Do you tend to think more about what you are getting or what you are paying? Do you embrace risk-taking? It may be that in calculating outcomes you weigh potential losses more heavily than potential gains. This bias can distort the cost-benefit analysis. So, too, can selective attention to the information available, being content with too little information, or insisting on more than is readily available or pertinent. In short, there are a number of ways this process can be short-circuited.

So why bother? If you are going to aim for results like a pro, then you should plan like one. A professional uses the best tools available and uses them appropriately. Cost-benefit analysis is just a tool. It is there to assist you, but it must keep its place. Properly, cost-benefit analysis is to help you invest wisely in yourself and in your goals. If you keep that in mind, then practice will help you to more and more use this tool both effectively and productively.

Dreaming

Professionals never forget to take time to remember why they are planning so carefully. They avoid becoming so entangled in the details that they lose sight of the larger picture. A real pro starts with a dream, a vision of what he or she wants to someday see. Then, step by careful step, they plan and build toward that dream. The reality of the work only partly keeps them grounded; the strength of the vision they hold keeps them most firmly rooted to their path.

What are your dreams? In the face of life's storms it is easy to quit dreaming. It seems like dreams are doomed to disappointment. Yet, we really can't stop dreaming. Even if our dreams take on a quality of pure fantasy to us, we can't quite give them up entirely. To live is to dream.

Give yourself permission to dream. Sit back, close your eyes, and imagine what you want. Picture yourself a year from now—five years from now—a decade. Who do you see? What are you doing? What is your life like?

Do it right. Really indulge in your dream. Don't worry about being practical or 'realistic.' What is both practical and realistic is to have a dream. Your dream provides you crucial motivational energy and a set of concrete goals.

Once you have that dream firmly in mind, then you can start drafting a blueprint of actions to move you from where you are to where you want to be. Humanistic psychologists like Carl Rogers use a similar approach in helping people effect desired changes in their process of becoming. To realize your full potential—to be the person you want to be—you must both be honest about who you are *and* have a clear image of the person you want to be. By measuring the distance between your 'real' self and your 'ideal' self, you can start gauging what steps you need to take to narrow the distance between them.

Setbacks, losses, disappointments and failures all offer new chances to start over in one or more respects. You have a brief window of opportunity to dream about what you want most in the days ahead and about who you want to become. Don't shortchange yourself! Now more than ever your dreams matter. They are a vital source of energy to fuel you as you struggle hip deep in the mud of the downpouring rain. They are a vision to guide you back into the warmth and light. Dream on.

Here is space to write down some dreams; be as detailed and expansive as you can be. The goal is a richly imagined set of dreams to pursue.

My Dreams

Step 3

Create New Knowledge and Skills

Effective action follows laying a personal foundation (step one), and sensible planning (step two). But it requires having the keys to open the doors you will be facing. I want to show you three keys. One you already have in your pocket. A second is in your hand right now, ready to be used. The third is available whenever you are ready to pick it up.

Each key reflects an element of time. The familiar lyric 'time is on your side' is correct. Though the damp darkness of the storm may make the present seem like endless misery and the future an impossibility, the truth is much different. Every part of time really is on your side, if only you can recognize the key each provides. These keys hold incredible power.

Through them you can create new knowledge and skills. In this manner you will be able to continue the building process you have begun. Through these keys you keep continuity with the best of your past, establish yourself in the present, and plan for the future. These three keys can open doors that right now may appear tightly locked. As you use them to unlock doors, and pass through, you will bring yourself step by step closer to the success you desire.

Right now, I can imagine you desperately want to believe me. Yet, you hold back. Skepticism, together with a natural fear of greater disappointment, makes you cautious. Good for you. Your trust in what I say should be earned. So let's do it.

Experience—the Key from the Past

The first key sits in your pocket right now. It has been there all along. Its shape and strength have been steadily growing. This key has a unique design of your own crafting. Right now it is very important to you, whether you know it or not.

You need this key to come out of your pocket and into your hand. It will help you through this difficult time. You cannot change whatever has happened. In that sense, the past remains a door closed to one and all. However, from that door comes a key, which can open other doors now and in the future. That key is *experience*.

I want you to take out this key and inspect it closely. Every bend, dent, nick and scratch has been earned. This can be a painful key to hold, especially right now. With rain in your eyes and mud beneath your feet this key can easily slip from your grasp to be covered in muck. But it belongs to you. In fact, it is yours alone. You are the only legitimate owner and the only one who can use it fully.

I am going to show you how to use this key. Whether you actually use it is up to you. The first thing I want you to do is to draw how you see this key. Do it now before reading any further. Here is some space for your drawing:

I grant this may appear a silly little exercise, but it has a purpose. By making a concrete image of how you see your experience as a key, you accomplish two important things. First, you make yourself see your experience as a key, which it really is. Second, your drawing offers you the chance to reflect on how you are presently evaluating your experience. So maybe it isn't so silly after all.

Let me explain a little bit more. Many psychologists think that our unconscious mind is revealed in our dreams, the stories and jokes we tell, and our drawings. What does your drawing suggest to you? Have you pictured a small key or a large one? Is it shiny or dirty? Is it a rather generic key or one filled with character? What does it say about you and how you view your accumulated experience? You might wish also to ask someone close to you to evaluate your drawing. He or she may be able to suggest things you cannot see. In this manner you can gain insight into your own way of thinking about yourself and your life.

Now I want you to reflect back on the doors this key has successfully opened in the past. Surround your drawing of your key with images of doors. Label each one. Then draw a line from your key to each door and write on the line a very brief description of how your key opened, or helped open that particular door.

Let me provide an example. My key of experience includes writing many, many, *many* pages. In the past, that experience helped open the door of a college education. By having so much practice writing before college I was better prepared than many of my fellow students for the writing I had to do in college. Later, that experience also helped me open the door to a graduate education. Still later it was useful in my writing a doctoral dissertation. Regardless of whatever talent I might have for writing, it was my actual experience of doing it that helped open important doors for me.

Do you see how your experience has helped you to many past successes? The doors opened may not be toweringly important to you, but they were closed at one time and it was your key that opened them. Never forget that. Your past success in opening closed doors, even if only relatively unimportant ones, proves you have the skill to do so now. In fact, I am certain you have opened some very important doors in the past. I know that experience can help you now.

Go back to your drawing. Create a new circle of doors outside the ones you have opened in the past. These new doors represent the obstacles you are facing, the challenges before you, and the dreams you have. Can you discover connections between doors opened in the past and ones in your present and future? A similarity between doors suggests that you can find in your experience what you need to apply this key right now.

Never underestimate what you have earned through experience. You have acquired a key to open what may at first appear as locked doors. Knowing how to sort through your experiences, and select the appropriate ones as needed, will get you through doors more swiftly. So take that key out of your pocket, grasp it firmly, and use it to your advantage.

Experimentation—the Key of the Present

Just as your past provides the first key, your actions today comprise a second key. Through *experimentation* you can extend your store of experience. This helps build your first key while actually using your second. Experimenting now can turn your sense of derailment into the excitement of being on a new track. Your journey isn't over—it may just have changed direction.

When we met at step one, I asked that we be honest about where we were meeting. Now I want you to be honest about this place you are in. Doesn't it, at least a little, send shivers of excitement up your spine? After all, welcome or not, painful as it is, hard as it is—you have a chance now at something new and different. Who knows if it won't be better than what you had before? The future isn't written and logically it is as reasonable to think the future will be better as it is to conclude it will be worse.

As long as change has been thrust upon you, take charge of that change. Use the energy of the storm to initiate some experiments. Now is the perfect time. Voluntarily change some of those things you have been meaning to change, but never quite got around to before. Take the attitude that as long as circumstances are going to play with you, you are going to play with them!

Fortune comes to us all. But only the brave embrace adversity. As my teacher Seneca said, "Without a foe, courage shrinks." We prove our virtue in rising to meet a fickle fortune with the resolute good intention to turn peril into advantage. The key to that transformation is in daring to experiment.

Start small. Begin with something manageable that you have wanted to do but put off. Perhaps it is introducing yourself to someone you have seen but never quite got around to greeting. Or maybe it is making a change in your personal appearance. It might be as simple as reading that book you were given, or rearranging a room. Whatever it is, now is the time to do it.

So what if you fail? Maybe the person you meet proves to be a snob. Perhaps you change your appearance and decide you liked the old you better. Some experiments fail. The point remains true that with nothing ventured, nothing can be gained.

But how do you do it? There are many different ways to experiment, and I hope you decide experimentation is worth doing many times. Still, there are certain elements shared by good experiments that are crucial to their success. These include:

1. Be clear about what you are interested in and what you want to learn.

2. Form a working statement about what you expect to find. (You can write it on page 35.) This is called a hypothesis and it is what your experiment will test.

3. Design your experiment carefully. Decide now, before you start, how long it will run, what tools you will need, and what steps you will take. (Write your details on page 35.)

4. Follow your plan as best you can. Give it a full effort.

5. When you are done, evaluate both your process and the results. If you failed, maybe it was because your process was somehow a little flawed. If you succeeded, perhaps you can follow a similar process to succeed at another experiment.

Experimentation teaches some important lessons. First, it proves to yourself that you can try new and different things. In the brave new world after the storm you are likely going to have to live differently so now is a good time to practice. Second, every time you experiment and fail you prove your survival skills. In fact, given enough failures, you will probably actually improve your survival skills and find that failing isn't as big a deal as it once seemed. Third, failed experiments can clarify what you really want—which may be different from what you thought when you started the experiment—and teach you valuable lessons for the next time around. When I fail at an experiment I don't automatically give up on the experiment; I can alter certain parts of it in accordance with what I have learned. Finally, experimenting sometimes succeeds! Then you have gained both experience and success.

Experimentation will reveal new doors to pass through. Perhaps the most wonderful aspect of experimentation is how it opens our eyes to possibilities. The process allows you to try out new paths, gain knowledge, and acquire new skills. All of these help develop you as a person.

If you haven't already done so, *please* take time now to draft your experiment on the next page. Remember to be as specific and detailed as you can.

My Experiment

Education—the Key to the Future

The key to the future is *education*. The pace of our modern world has created an age where lifelong learning is more than a clever slogan schools use to attract students—it is an essential tool for staying apace of change and at the front of the crowd. Most students grasp that a college education is important for their career earnings potential. But education ultimately means much more than a better job and higher income.

We should know this from life itself. We are always in one classroom or another. Most of us can confess that we have learned some of our most important lessons in the school of hard knocks. In fact, in psychology perhaps the most common definition for 'learning' is 'a relatively permanent change due to experience.' The ancient Latins summed up lifelong learning in the very brief phrase *'experientia docet'*—experience teaches. But what is it you resolve to learn?

Education offers the opportunity to make of yourself a better person. In fact, the university originated as an institution for the improvement of the human being. I still think that should be its basic objective. I have never been bashful about telling my students I am interested far more in their exiting the course a better person than I am in their remembering everything about the subject. I ask that you regard education as learning how to be a better human being.

The fact is, nothing is more important. If your storm right now is a crisis, remember what you are learning can make you more human than you have ever been. Your suffering can be a crucible for appreciating the pathos we are all capable of experiencing. It can also offer opportunities to transcend your grief in creative expressions of your experience. And as you grow, you will become the kind of human being who attracts other more fully realized people. In resolving to learn how to grow through your loss you will find yourself surrounded by strong people who have learned in their own unique ways the same important lessons.

When I lost my job, I determined to learn what I could from the experience. I wanted not only to not repeat the experience, but also to wrest from it everything beneficial I could find. I was determined to find ways to become a better person. Of course, that is easier said than it was done. I felt weakened by the experience and questioned myself severely. Many days I was angry at my weakness and seeming inability to grow and develop like I wanted.

I was impatient. Every student is at some point. You will be too. But good things come to those who patiently persevere. Learning is a matter not only of paying attention, but of doing so repetitively. Most things have to happen over and over before they really sink in.

As the key to the future, you can resolve to learn through both formal and informal channels. For example, if your disappointments come in relationships, read books and articles on the subject, take time to observe successful ones, and talk to people who you think have learned the lessons you want to master. Whatever your storm is, you must be the student who researches its characteristics and discovers the best ways to weather it.

Opportunities for learning abound. Educational avenues surround you. If money is an obstacle, consider free courses offered by nonprofit groups. Most churches offer educational programs and some are extensive. Local colleges may provide continuing education classes where new skills can be gained without too much expense or time commitment. And this might be the right time to go back to school for a more formal course of training. Perhaps a degree is in your future.

Be of good cheer. You have taken this key to the future in hand already. By reading this book and following its steps you are pursuing an education. You are learning about yourself. You are becoming the person you want to be.

Perhaps in this space you can list other books you want to read or classes you want to take:

Books

Classes

Step 4.

Diversify!

The keys of the previous chapter perhaps alerted you to the genuine importance of being a well-rounded generalist. Experience, experimentation, and education all point toward the need to be flexible and competent in many things. The reason is simple: life is complex. To meet life challenges, especially the darker ones, requires a wide set of skills. In a rapidly changing world, those who diversify their personal attributes and their work skills have the best chance of moving ahead and coping with the stressful pressures of life.

You probably have heard the word 'diversification' in connection with the stock market. Investors are urged to diversify their portfolio. The logic is compelling. Diversifying balances your financial prospects, protects against undue risk, and provides greater opportunities for profit. Personal diversification does all these same things.

Since you want to prosper both personally and professionally, you need to see the connection between the two spheres. Professional success is built on personal growth. In today's fast paced world, where change is both constant and rapid, diversification is essential. Today, most people will have more than one career during their lifetime. This reality not only makes lifelong learning necessary, it requires a flexibility of mind and an adaptive personality.

Success has always been linked to broad personal interests, sound basic skills in speaking and writing, and proficient people skills. We live in a world where success is connected to other people. Their perception is critical. Your ability to cope with widely differing personalities and styles is critical, too. Though relating to others—especially 'the public'—can be frustrating and difficult, no success either personally or professionally is likely without finding positive ways to manage the process.

Later, in step eight, we will focus on the task of connecting with others. Right now we want to keep your focus on the Self you are building. Everything you have done so far has made this step possible. You know who you are, you appreciate yourself, you know your assets, you have planned like a pro, and you hold the keys to open doors to greater success.

With the good work you have done so far, maybe you are seeing that the storm won't last forever. In fact, I am betting that the effort you have put in so far means you are feeling better, thinking more clearly, and sensing an end to the rain. You have earned these changes by making yourself do healthy things. Stormy weather can entice us into hunkering down and battening the hatches. But you have stuck your neck out. You have proven already an ability to be flexible, adaptive, and proactive.

The next step is to use what you have developed in a conscious effort to become more diverse. In a sense, this means rejoining the world as a cosmopolitan citizen. You can become someone comfortable in many different settings and circumstances. Your new diversity will build your confidence and present you with many new, as yet unforeseen, opportunities.

Personal diversification means learning some new ABCs to continue improving your self-language skills. Any cosmopolitan citizen must be able to speak many languages in order to communicate effectively while moving from one country to another. In a similar fashion, you must master a number of different alphabets, each with its own vocabulary, to meet different challenges. The very act of doing this work is diversifying you!

Adapt

The first letter in the strategy to diversify is 'A' for *adapt*. Let me be clear what I mean by adaptation. Your storm has produced a new set of life circumstances. It has altered your environment. You need to find ways to survive in this environment. Adapting means changing yourself to be suitable for success in your changed circumstances. This doesn't mean selling out or giving up. You can be adaptive and remain true to your values; adaptation is not mere accommodation.

As always, it is easier to say this than it is to do it. In fact, I don't blame you for thinking, 'It's easy enough for Bolich to talk!' You may have concluded that if you are reading this book, then I must be sitting comfortably amidst my riches. The more accurate—and relevant—perception would be to realize that in writing this book I am putting into practice the very steps I am offering to you. Losing my position in academia provided me with incentive to diversify my own person and portfolio. Sharing what I learned with you is one way I am growing and broadening myself.

Adapting to change can take many paths; every storm presents unique challenges. However, the *process* of adaptation is similar enough across situations that several key elements can be identified. By recognizing them, you can see better the course to follow for yourself. Here they are:

- Adapting entails emotional adjustment.

- Adapting requires what some psychologists call 'cognitive reframing,' or changing the way you think about certain things.

- Adapting means altering behavior to fit new needs.

- Finally, adapting always means finding solutions to specific problems, solutions that contribute to success—not failure.

In sum, adapting means positive changing in the direction of growth and for the purpose of enhanced success. Seen in that light, adapting looks pretty attractive, doesn't it?

There remains the practical problem of accomplishing adaptation. Let's take each basic element in the process and see how you can profit from it.

Emotional adjustment is perhaps the first requirement of adaptation and the hardest to muster. Storms hit us in the gut. I had trouble getting past the unfairness of what happened to me. Whatever feelings plague you, they probably seem highly resistant to change. Let me suggest you try three things that might alleviate some of the pain and facilitate the adjustment you know you need:

- Isolate the feelings. What this entails is setting aside a specific time each day to experience these feelings fully. Then, during the remainder of the day, as the feelings surface and demand attention, choke them off with the reminder to yourself that you have wisely set aside time for them— and now is not that time.

- Compete with the feelings. Too often when we are troubled by anger, disappointment, bitterness or other strong negative emotion, we add to our troubles. We disallow ourselves to feel anything else. What you need to do is to encourage positive feelings. Don't just give yourself permission to feel good at times, actively promote those sensations!

- Give yourself time. Strong feelings can be very resistant to change because they signify an ongoing troubling state. Once fully engaged, our emotional system can take a long time to settle.

Cognitive reframing, or changing the way you think about certain things, will also aid you in your emotional adjustment. Reframing can be accomplished by doing some of the very things you have been accomplishing in these steps. In addition, try some of these things:

- Eliminate universal terms like 'always' and 'never,' and absolute terms like 'can't.' In adapting, where things are in flux, universal and absolute terms are inevitably inaccurate. You cannot truthfully say before trying something new, "I *can't* do this!" (an absolute assertion), because you don't really know. Your assumption is hurting you. Likewise, your saying 'I *always* screw up' is inaccurate—even if by accident you are bound to occasionally do something right.

- Practice thinking like a scientist. Every time you come up with an explanation for why something is happening, make yourself consider alternative possibilities. Thus, for example, when you fail to solve a particular problem and scream at yourself that the reason is you are a failure, look for other possible causes, such as not being adequately prepared, finding unexpected opposition, or simply being unlucky that one time.

- Learn to exaggerate your way out of cognitive myopia. When you are in the mood to insist on being irrational—using negative and absolute terms, limiting yourself to a single negative explanation—then permit yourself to go all the way. For instance, when someone turns you down on something, say to yourself, 'Well, that figures. I always blow it and never win. It's because I can't do anything right. I'm a failure. In fact, I'm such a creep that this person is probably on their way to the police right now to report me. Soon I'll be on my way to jail, where every news crew in the state will be ready to film my humiliation. The judge will throw the book at me—I'll probably get a death sentence!' Before long you will sheepishly smile at your nonsense—and be ready to move on.

Altering behavior reflects a sober recognition that when things aren't working it is time to try something different. Amazingly, as obvious as that is, most of us find it very hard to do. Try these suggestions to help you change how you act:

- Break down your behavior into the habits and patterns you suspect might be causing problems. Ask someone who knows you well to help by being candid (and really listen to them!).

- Imagine a different way of doing something. Ask for suggestions if you need to. Brainstorm. Then, after coming up with a variety of ideas, try one that is just a little different. There is nothing wrong in starting with incremental change before trying drastic change.

- Once you settle on trying something new, don't be halfhearted. Do it with your best effort. Give it a fair shot. Judge the results as objectively as you can. Again, ask someone you trust to give you an outside opinion. Fine tune as needed.

The final element, *finding solutions to specific problems*, is the very essence of adaptation. The first three elements all exist to make this one possible and successful. Or, to put it another way, the first three demand personal and internal changes so that we can accomplish public and external changes. We change so that we can solve the problems we need to solve to reach the success we want.

Here are three ways you can adaptively meet problems:

- Don't see problems where none exist ('don't fix the wheel if it isn't broken'), but do see ones that do exist. Problem identification is itself the first step to problem solving.

- Make the problem manageable. In other words, realize big problems take time to resolve. Break the problem into smaller chunks so you can see your success a bit at a time.

- Focus on progress rather than on a product. Success is not an all-or-nothing proposition. Take your wins where you can.

We will return to the matter of problem solving at step nine.

Finally, remember that adapting now is just part of a larger process. Your immediate objective is to cope with your present situation. But a crucial long-term goal needs to be diversifying yourself so that adaptation becomes easier and better. Skill at adapting builds success at staying current with many changes. Being proactive is far better than scrambling to survive.

Become

If adapting serves the greater purpose of diversifying yourself, what purpose does diversifying serve? Interestingly, diversity promotes *becoming*—the second letter in our new alphabet. I am speaking of the kind of becoming where you continually reach beyond yourself, growing toward your full potential, and realizing more of the total human experience. In this becoming, the future imperative of being all you can be directs your adaptation in the present. It propels you to survive now so that you can thrive later.

'Becoming' is what a philosopher or theologian might term a 'teleological' experience. This delightful Greek word means a concern with and direction toward some purpose, end, and design. Your becoming is not meant to be accidental in nature. You should cultivate seeing in your life an unfolding design toward some ultimate purpose.

Take responsibility for having a vision for your future. I don't mean tactical planning, where you figure out what to do next. I'm referring to strategic planning, where you have a broad and encompassing dream of who you can be and what you can accomplish. This kind of planning sees the full picture of what your life can mean. Your dream now will fuel the energy you need as you become what you dream.

Obviously, becoming means being in process. You have *not* arrived, no matter what your past successes or current problems may be telling you. If you are hearing the past and present correctly, you know you are on the way. The question is, *where are you headed?*

Take a moment right now to reflect on what your life means. Do this in two ways. First, see your diversifying yourself as part of the process of becoming. Ask these kinds of questions:

- How does expanding my range of interests help me become the person I desire to be?

- How will broadening my skills help me realize what I am seeing as my purpose in life?

- How can I make developing my personality assist my becoming all I am meant to be?

Here is some space to write your answers:

You can come up with other such questions. Ask them in order to clarify your direction and suggest the practical steps you will want to take.

Next, see your becoming as part of the process of diversifying. That's right—becoming is not just the goal of diversifying, it is also an aspect of it. Ask these kinds of questions:

- What new directions is my development taking me?

- Where am I showing new growth through new interests, new insights, new skills, and new efforts?

- How can I find new ways in which to let myself expand and diversify?

Here is some space to write down your answers:

New Directions:

New Growth:

New Ways to Expand & Diversify:

Generating questions like these is useful in promoting a self-dialog that will guide you along your path.

Finally, there is a potent danger you need to be aware of. Unless you are developing your own personhood, you stand in danger of reducing yourself to an object others will use and discard. Diversifying means becoming your fullest expression of the self you can be.

Change

We have come to our last letter in this short alphabet. 'C' is for *change*. Of course, unwanted and uninvited change is probably what brought me to your doorstep. You have already found change happening *to* you. Now make it happen *for* you.

But first, face facts. Some changes in life are inevitable—like changes in functioning as we grow older—and other changes are unintended, like accidents. Those we have to live with—and we can. Yet many changes are self-initiated. We don't have to just let change happen. In fact, we *don't*. Unfortunately, we tend to diminish our own capacity to make change by focusing on the changes that happen without our willing them.

It is critical to see yourself as a change-maker. You make changes regularly. Whether they are minor or not, they are worth looking at closely. They can show you both how to tackle bigger changes and remind you how good you are at making changes you want. So do this:

1. Challenge yourself to list at least two dozen changes, large and small, you have successfully made in your life. Use the space on the next page.

2. Now examine the list and analyze it. Write down any patterns you see, such as the kinds of changes you like to make or the way in which you make them.

3. Rate your satisfaction with these changes. If you can match certain rates of success and satisfaction with definite kinds of changes or methods you have used, then you have learned something very useful.

My Change List

1.	13.
2.	14.
3.	15.
4.	16.
5.	17.
6.	18.
7.	19.
8.	20.
9.	21.
10.	22.
11.	23.
12.	24.

Patterns I See

Now, consider changes you have experienced that you did *not* initiate. List several—painful though they may be—and ask yourself how you responded to them.

1.

My response was . . .

2.

My response was . . .

3.

My response was . . .

Using comparison and contrast with the changes you initiated you can learn how your responses to the different kinds of change work. You may find some similarities and some important differences. Then you can focus on adjusting your less successful responses.

Once you better understand your own existing way of managing change, you can improve it. Not all change is adaptive—but your aim is to make the changes you are responsible for as adaptive as possible. You can muster the will you need to do this—and you must if you are to realize the greater success you crave. Here are some ways to make your resolve effectual:

- Embrace change rather than resist it. See change as an opportunity to participate in the essence of living.

- Be persistent. Change can be hard but living with the results of not changing when you need to can be harder.

- Remember—and follow—the prayer of serenity: 'God, grant me the courage to change the things I can, to accept the things I can't change, and wisdom to know the difference.'

Remember, often the most important facts of life are the most obvious. Maybe that is why they are so easily overlooked. Here is one such obvious fact: change is inevitable in life. You know it. The issue is what you are going to do about it. The bottom line is probably obvious as well. You will best serve your own interests by learning to embrace and create change in the service of adaptation and becoming.

Step 5.

Embrace Opportunities

When I lost my job, I became acquainted with the Employment Securities Commission. The helpful folk there guided me through the new experience of filing an unemployment claim. As I received unemployment checks I was engaged in a work search. The ESC assisted my efforts by supplying useful information and notifying me of any job openings in my field that were reported to them. I kept a work search record and reported regularly to the local office.

During my storm, the ESC offered a temporary shelter. The experience was instructive to me. In the midst of tremendous insecurity, a rope had been thrown to me. As I reflected on this marvelous lifeline, it occurred to me that anyone can establish a personal security agency, not just for emergency self-assistance, but also for ongoing self-help. Just as employers pay into the system that supports the ESC, we can enhance our personal security by investing in developing ourselves.

In this step you will build your own ESC. Regardless of the setbacks or disappointments you experience in life, you can create some security to see you through. Even better, this personal ESC will provide an ongoing buffer against the slings and arrows of outrageous fortune. It will offer you ongoing protection. For this plan, ESC refers to essential elements in seeing and seizing opportunities. Accustoming yourself to collecting opportunities to succeed will both help you manage setbacks and pursue greater life success.

Why are seeing and seizing opportunities so critical to your personal security? As we have discussed, ours is a rapidly changing world. The weather systems that constitute our lives in such a world are more unpredictable than ever. Storms can strike at any time as change washes over us. We are no longer afforded the luxury of putting ourselves into a narrow life track and settling into a half-century career. Unless we learn to find and embrace opportunities, we not only limit ourselves, we take on an unacceptable risk level.

The essence of security lies in always knowing you have attractive alternatives you can pursue. Since you are committed to personal growth and development, cultivating alternatives means the security of knowing that whatever comes your way represents new opportunities along other paths. Rain from storms just means fuel for growth. Professionally, knowing you can succeed at more than one thing supplies the confidence to cope with setbacks. If one road forward is blocked, another skill can carry you down a different road of opportunity.

Eliminate Excuses

Your own personal ESC plan requires making an investment in yourself and in your future. The first element, 'E,' is for *eliminating excuses*. Your first move must be to stop finding reasons why you can't do something. Believe me, you will find it easy enough to explain why you can't try this or that. But that won't get you anywhere. Learning how to identify and eliminate excuses will make you a responsible taskmaster to yourself.

This may seem a small element. In reality, I think it is the largest and most difficult for many of us. Excuses do more than prevent investing in ourselves. They actually serve as withdrawals from our own personal accounts. They diminish our confidence, undermine our actions, and discourage our allies.

Most of us are perfectly aware of when we are making excuses. We may even know why. But if you are having some trouble identifying your excuses, consider what I call the '7 Perils of Self-persuasion':

1. *Problems*—you excuse yourself from looking for new opportunities because you are completely wrapped up in your present difficulties. While it is prudent to pay attention to problems, solving them generally means actively considering alternatives.

2. *Pain*—you may be suffering so much from your setback that your pain blinds all else—or so you say. But after a certain point, wallowing in pain is just an excuse to stay inactive. Or your looking for new opportunities may itself be painful. Stretching generally is uncomfortable at first. In this case, it really is true, 'no pain, no gain.'

3. *Panic*—the idea of doing something different generates anxiety for most people. An impending sense of panic—the erroneous feeling that there are no alternatives, or you can't find them, or you won't succeed anyway—may lurk behind your rationalizations.

4. *Paralysis*—you see so many possibilities you don't know where to head first. So you don't move at all. Or, you feel so overwhelmed or incompetent that you don't dare move for fear of falling further than you have already.

5. *Priorities*—your priorities may need adjustment. You are in a new reality. Where you may have thought you had the luxury of ignoring opportunities before, the new need means bumping up such searching toward the head of the list. Sometimes, excuses not to act reflect the reality that

the action is simply not felt important enough. The problem is motivation. In this case, you may have to sink into a state of utter desperation before you do what was sensible from the start.

6. *Perfectionism*—you may sense how hard it can be to succeed in new ventures like you did in old ones. It may be tempting to hold back because if you suffered a setback in what you thought you did well, how much riskier must it be to try something new? It does take time to master new skills, new learning, new behaviors. But if you wait to be perfect at something before trying it, how will you ever try anything?

7. *Procrastination*— you may be plagued by what is perhaps the most common of the seven perils. How easy it is to just delay. Often, one of the other six perils supply the energy for procrastination. In any event, delaying the inevitable does not make the inevitable any less inevitable!

As you can see, excuse making can mask powerful forces. Your excuses may be resting on compelling reasons, though those reasons are self-defeating.

So how do you triumph over these obstacles? How can you learn to effectively overcome your excuses? Here's how:

*   Know yourself. Know your personality tendencies, your excuses, and your fears.

*   Argue with yourself. Contest your excuses. Unmask and disarm them.

*   Challenge your excuses with action. If you can't sell yourself on a big step, take a small one. Act in spite of your excuses and you soon will simply spite them!

You may never stop *making* excuses, but you can stop *obeying* them.

See Opportunities

Now that you have arrested your habit of making withdrawals through excuses, it is time to make some deposits. Every opportunity you find and every alternative you explore is like putting money in the bank against another inevitable stormy day. You are building precious resources. Thus, the second element in your personal SEC plan is 'S,' for *seeing opportunities.*

Open your eyes. I know how failure and loss cover our eyes with mist. But like the Apostle Paul, we must have the scales drop from our eyes and really see the opportunities that surround us. It is a blessed irony that so-called 'setbacks' inevitably widen the field of opportunity rather than narrow it. They urge us to lift our eyes from the path we were on and look around like we were seeing things for the first time.

Opportunities abound. We just have to see them. Consider these potential sources:

- your neighborhood;

- community centers;

- local schools (high schools, community colleges, universities, etc.);

- places of worship (churches, synagogues, mosques, temples); and,

- special events (fairs, community gatherings, etc.).

And these barely scratch the surface. All of them are rich repositories. Some provide comfort and aid in time of need. All are banks of opportunities for making new personal contacts, volunteering your services, finding assistance programs, and learning about many different kinds of opportunities.

Knowing *where* to look is important. Know *what* to look for is the next thing. Many opportunities are missed because we aren't clear inside ourselves what we are looking for. In the ESC plan you are developing, it is vital to develop resources for the future as well as looking for ways out of the present storm.

Here are a few tips:

1. Review steps 1-4 and reaffirm or adjust as needed. In those steps you looked honestly at yourself, counted your assets, planned wisely, and set an agenda for your development. Use your insights to guide your search for opportunities.

2. Create a list of opportunities you *want* to find. (There is space provided on the next page.) Be sure to include opportunities for your character development as well as professional advancement. Order your wish list in descending order of importance. Don't worry about whether some items are unrealistic—it's a wish list! Then start exploring, going through the list one at a time, but keeping your eyes open to everything on it.

3. Add to your wish list those kinds of opportunities you are willing to accept even if they aren't what you most want. Consider these 'stepping-stone' options that you will pursue because they have something to teach you, they meet an immediate need and expand your portfolio, and they can advance your progress toward the opportunities you most want.

On the following page I have provided space for you to produce your wish list, but before you do that, *please* remember to use the above tips. If you find the creation of this list is not pleasurable, pause and think about that. Doing this should be enjoyable because it is offering you the chance to express your desires. If you are still too wet to enjoy this, perhaps you need more time to review the earlier steps. This one will still be here when you are ready to move forward. I don't want you to do this just to be doing it. Do it because it matters—and enjoy.

My Wish List

1.

2.

3.

4.

5.

6.

7.

8.

9.

10.

As you become experienced in seeing opportunities, you will develop better vision—you'll be clearer about what to look for. I suggest keeping a book with a list of tips for yourself. Blank books are available at many stores and are ideal for such a use. Or, if you prefer, keep such tips in a diary.

Now that the 'where' and 'what' are answered, there remain the 'how' and the 'why.' *How* you see opportunities actually entails two dimensions. First, there are the practical mechanics of finding them. Second, there is the inward disposition you hold toward what you find. Let's look briefly at each.

A practical method for finding opportunities extends beyond knowing where to look and what to look for. It includes the actual practical mechanics of searching. When I was considering how to proceed, I followed certain definite steps that proved very useful. Here is what I did—and what you can do, too:

- I turned to my allies—the people I knew supported me—explained my situation, shared my dreams, and solicited their feedback. They pointed out alternatives I was unaware of and some I hadn't seriously considered. They offered support for my efforts to grow through my pain. In providing me truly honest information about myself, such as where I needed to grow, helpful tips about contacts and openings, these friends and family members greatly aided me.

- I read—anything and everything I could get my hands on. I read newspapers, magazines, books, and internet websites. Some were to help me weather the storm, but all of them were potential doors into new ways of thinking, feeling, and behaving. They provided opportunities for acquiring new insights, developing new skills, and finding alternative courses of action.

- I got out into the world and tried to see it like I never had before. I observed people. I went places I had not been in a long time, and even some new ones. And absolutely everywhere I went I asked myself how this place could help me in my quest. I was forcing myself to *see*.

As you may have realized, everything in the mechanics is about a heroic quest. You gather companions, share a vision, and start walking, always open for unexpected aid. The mechanics of seeing opportunities are those of living: using your eyes, ears, hands and feet. It isn't a mystery and there are no secrets. Rather, it is a grand adventure.

That point leads to the other half of how you seek opportunities. Your regard for your search and for what you find is crucial. If your attitude is to demean the task, or what you see, or yourself, then the value of the opportunity is greatly diminished. You don't need dread, but excitement. An opportunity represents a chance to succeed. Seize it!

Finally, answering *why* you should look for opportunities and find them has been answered already. I wanted the excuse to recall your attention to this because it is so important. In seeing opportunities you are committing yourself to building a more secure future. You are cultivating your responsibility for yourself and enhancing your personal freedom.

Collect Chances to Succeed

Only one element remains. Yet the plan fails without this element. After eliminating excuses and learning to see opportunities, you still must do something with those opportunities. 'C' is for *collecting chances to succeed*. This entails the art of turning sight into acquisition.

In some respects, this can be the easiest element. You may be highly motivated. After a disappointment in life it is natural to want in one large step to return to the level of success you had before. You may be eager to grasp for the big brass ring.

But why aim so low? Is matching previous success what you really want? If you want greater success, then I urge you to consider something other than a big leap. Collecting lots of small opportunities can build to greater success than you ever imagined. Being in a process for the long haul can produce greater profit than an all-or-nothing approach.

Collecting chances to succeed means making calculated deposits in your personal account. These deposits are actual acquisitions. Some are things you learn. Others are new skills. They can be personal—attributes of character you develop, or professional—new ventures and audiences to serve. Here are some of the ways to collect chances to succeed:

- Keep a list of opportunities, whether personal or professional. Personal opportunities might include a chance to learn something you have always been interested in. Professional ones might include new areas in which to expand your expertise or ventures.

- When you find an opportunity, explore it. Learn as much as you can in a reasonable length of time. Even if the opportunity does not pan out, the knowledge you acquired may help out down the road.

- Visualize an opportunity as comprised of several smaller opportunities. If the overall opportunity seems to exceed your grasp right now, reach for one of the smaller opportunities that are a part of it. By taking it on, and succeeding, you extend your reach.

- See *everything* as an opportunity for success. Keep records of new ideas, new learning, new skills, new experiences, and new relationships. Learn to stay active in such a manner that you are constantly turning what you see into a chance to build your success.

- Bit by bit these deposits will make you rich.

Try practicing by listing a half dozen opportunities you can at least imagine may be open to you:

1.

2.

3.

4.

5.

6.

Security and freedom need not be rivals. In embracing opportunities, you build security at the same time you expand your personal freedom. In broadening the person you are and what you can do, you make yourself more secure against being thrown seriously off balance. Simultaneously, you experience the exhilaration of stretching yourself toward your potential. Ultimately, there is no greater security than exercising your freedom to develop yourself fully.

You now have the elements of a personal ESC plan. You can build toward a secure future. In that future, you will be finding reasons to succeed rather than explaining why you can't. You will be finding opportunities all around. You will be grasping those opportunities, building yourself and your dream. What could be more liberating?

Step 6.

Face Forward and Focus

Congratulations! You have taken five very important steps toward greater success. You are now halfway through the process for self-development and personal growth this little book advocates. You should feel pride and a sense of accomplishment. You have proven the storm has not mastered you. The brightness of sunnier days beckons.

Here at the midpoint is a good place to implement the Janus Plan. In mythology, Janus was generally represented by the figure of a gatekeeper holding a staff and key. He had two heads, facing in opposite directions. Early associated with the light of the sun, he came to be the patron deity of all comings and goings. He was the deity of beginnings and of gates.

Every gate faces two directions and so does this moment you now are in. As you walk through the storm it is only natural to look back to drier, warmer days. A sense of longing, perhaps of regret, can fill you as the memories come. Unfortunately, it is tempting to focus on what you have lost rather than what you have left. Looking ahead can be hard when the present and future are measured in scales holding the weight of past losses in the counterbalance.

As we have journeyed, I have asked you to periodically look back at earlier steps. I want you to experience a growing sense of progress as you build toward ever increasing success. In truth, advancing to greater success frequently follows stepping back, pausing, and regathering strength. But the looking behind needs to be very teleological—purposeful, designed, and focused on an end. Looking back is meant to show you how far you have come so that you are not overwhelmed by how far you still have to travel.

The Janus Plan provides an orientation to help you manage your ongoing journey. It offers a way at every moment to face both backwards and forwards. Its purpose is to coordinate this double gaze into the single process of facing forward and focusing on your goal. By using the Janus Plan you can face both your fears and the facts so that you can move ahead with confidence. You will learn to look back in order to help you face forward.

The Janus Plan helps you put on two faces as you confront life. It does not matter how you feel when you put them on. Think of them as masks. You put them on and conform your behavior to them. Their purpose is to help you at every gate and new beginning. At such places and times your two faces will assist you as you meet the face of Fortune.

Face Your Fears

Your first mask is a brave face as you confront your fears. They are rooted in past experience and mirrored in future uncertainty. Though it may be hardest to be brave after a storm has frightened you, perhaps even knocking the stuffing out of you, it is imperative to face your fears. If you don't, your vision will be limited. Fears put blinders on you by keeping you from looking at things you need to see. In turn, what you don't see you cannot effectively handle. You may even find you feel paralyzed and cannot move at all. Looking brave is the first step to acting brave. It gets you moving again so that you can begin overcoming your fears.

As is so often the case, facing fears is easier said than done. The obstacle to overcome is obvious: fears are scary! When I lost my job all the wolves I had held at bay inside myself came out in force. They howled my insecurities full throat at me until all I wanted was to cower with my hands over my ears and my eyes tightly shut. Yet I could still hear them, and even with my eyes closed I could see them. In trying to shut them out I only succeeded in closing them in with me so that all I was aware of was the fear they generated. I couldn't see anything in the future but the specters of the past.

Almost always, the problem lies not in knowing what our fears are, but in facing them. My fears came from the dark woods of my past and the illusion filled shadows of my future. The past howled that it proved I was never going to amount to anything. The future growled its agreement, arguing that if I had failed once I surely would again. The past told me all my efforts at being good, at working hard and honestly meant nothing—and again my future fears concurred. The incessant baying surrounded me.

You know at least some of your fears. Though you may not wish to face them, you can at least name them. The ancients believed that to name a thing asserted authority over it. I agree. The first movement in facing your fears is simply to name them.

Take a sheet of paper—any old scrap will do—and name as many fears as you can. Some will reflect what your past is howling, while others will be growls from an uncertain future. Don't do anything more than name them. Confession is good for the soul and you will feel better having them sitting there as objects on a piece of paper.

Now look at the words. They are just words—letters arranged on a silly little scrap. You can reach down at any time, pick up the paper, wad it up and throw it away. Or, you can tear it to pieces. Or, you can set it afire and watch it reduced to a small pile of ash. Go ahead—do it. You'll like it.

Maybe you feel better now, but you know it was just a game. The real fears are more than words. They still lurk all about you. You can avoid them for a time, but in the quiet night they steal upon your sleep. It is still too easy to cower.

The Janus Plan got me up, and moving again. I won't claim it was easy. I was scared and my knees shook as I stood up. But if I was going to deal with wolves, I knew I had to do something. So I put on the mask of bravery and pretended what I did not feel.

This is what I did—and what you can also do:

1. I made a decision that I had suffered enough.

2. Since the wolves of my fears weren't going away, I had to, which meant *I* had to do the moving.

3. Because I was surrounded by my fears, I knew whatever direction I moved, I had to go through some of them. So I resolved to move the direction I wanted. In essence, I chose which fears I would face first.

4. Though scared the wolves would devour me, I steeled myself, set my jaw, put on the mask of bravery, and took my first step. I acted brave.

The mask was a tool. By using it I was able to start doing what I needed to do. Eventually, I could take the mask off and the face underneath looked the same. I could face my fears. And so can you.

In psychology we have developed techniques to help people overcome the kind of severe fears we know as phobias. The most widely used tool is probably 'progressive, systematic desensitization.' Just as the name promises, it is a process that follows a plan step-by-step to lessen the fear until it is manageable. Your goal is not to eliminate your fears, but to face them. That means being able to manage your behavior despite your fear's threatening presence.

You can pursue a form of this treatment at home. You can attempt it by yourself, but I recommend enlisting the help of someone you feel comfortable talking to about personal issues. Tell your friend that his or her role is a limited one. Your friend is to listen, not offer advice. You have responsibility for your own life—including your fears—and you must not give that responsibility to anyone else.

Your self-treatment will proceed according to the following steps (the progressive plan to desensitize you):

1. Name your fears. You have done this already so this step should be easy. This time I have provided space for you to list them. (Someday you will look back and these won't seem so frightening after all.) As you name them, rate your fear on a scale of 1-10, with 10 being absolutely terrified and with 1 being completely comfortable. Anything below a 5 is an honest acknowledgment it still isn't pleasant, but it *is* manageable. Name your fears as often as you need until your rating is low (4 or less).

My Fears (and their rating on a scale from 1-10)

-

-

-

-

-

2. Select one fear at a time and start talking about it. Rate how uncomfortable this is on the 1-10 scale. Keep talking about it until your fear level is reduced to the manageable levels (below 5). You can talk about the sensations the fear creates, the problems it presents, how it affects you—anything so long as it centers your attention on the fear until it is diminished. Your friend may help by asking you questions.

3. Staying focused on the same fear as before, talk about how you see it relating to your future. Rate your discomfort. You may have talked about this before, but do it again. This time, brainstorm things you can do to confront the fear by specific behaviors you can try. Keep doing this until you have several suggestions and your fear level is manageable.

4. Select one of the suggestions you made last time and try it. Actually do the behavior. Rate yourself as you start and persist in doing it until the fear is manageable. Congratulations—you are on the move.

5. Repeat the process with other fears until it becomes an automatic habit. Constant, direct confrontation of your fears makes you gradually insensitive to them. It allows you more focus as you face forward.

Do it right by taking as much time as you need. Each step above is envisioned as a separate session lasting about an hour. If you are serious with the task, even an hour a week can bring a dramatic reduction in your level of fear in a few weeks. You can combine steps in a single session if you wish. Be guided by the effectiveness you achieve.

Face the Facts

I find it is helpful in facing my fears to use one other mask. Like Janus, I can wear two faces at the same time. The other face, or mask, is a sober one. The eyes are wide open, staring intensely. The brow is furrowed in concentration. The face is set to face the facts, whatever they might be.

Facing facts can prove to be as difficult as facing fears. It entails everything we have discussed in the steps so far—and more. It also means facing all the obstacles and opportunities in a realistic *and* optimistic manner. Because you have been learning to do this through the previous steps, we can concentrate here on adding some new ideas.

Let me start with a saying of statisticians: 'figures don't lie, but liars figure.' Even 'facts' are susceptible to misuse. In facing facts correctly you need to aim at objectivity by letting the facts be themselves rather than what you want them to be. Rigorous honesty with the facts can help guard you against self-deception. Having command of the facts can enable you to plan more effectively, act more confidently, and face forward with focus.

Here are the key ideas for facing facts:

- Facts are *always* on your side. Even if they bring unwelcome news, it is better to have them than to be ignorant of them. Your fears and other feelings have to take a back seat.

- Facts are tools. They are selected and manipulated. In facing facts, you are not merely trying to see them as they are, you are trying to find ways to use them.

The difference between facing fears and facing facts may be that with the former we are trying to get past a distraction while with the latter we are trying to find help for the future. In both cases, we want to be free to focus our energies forward. Facing facts correctly is an optimistic task because it recognizes the twin truths named above. It marshals the power of facts into the service of our dreams.

There are many ways to use facts to facilitate a forward focus. Here are a few:

- Make facts the frontline soldiers in your battle against fears. Confront fears—which tend to become irrational as they grow—with facts concerning your strength, resources (including allies), and abilities.

- Marshall facts to confront *any* negative emotion. Feelings offer information, and matter, but they aren't facts. When, for instance, you are feeling discouraged, point out facts that give you reason to hope for a brighter future.

- Use facts to sort out sense from nonsense. If you can't substantiate something with well-grounded data, then it is probably nonsense.

- List facts that support the direction you want to move. These are highly relevant facts and provide capital for your investment in yourself. Build on them by extending them. As you do so, you will both be adding new facts and actually moving the direction you desire.

- Balance the facts that suggest you can't do something by reappraising them and setting other facts beside them. You don't have to ignore facts pointing to obstacles to overcome because they are useful in getting you where you want to go. So you can reevaluate them as allies. They have spied out the land before you and shown you the potential ambushes. But be sure to also see the facts that you'll draw on to get over the problems (such as the fact of your resolve, the fact of how carefully you have planned, and the facts of your various assets).

Clearly, the facts are on your side.

Face Fortuna

Now you can face Fortune. The ancients called her Fortuna, the deity associated with chance and good luck, but also with fertility and family. In short, the ancients saw Fortune as the open future where all things are possible, including the best life has to offer. Your attitude toward Fortune—and the future—needs to mirror your masks. Be brave and face facts—Fortune may seem arbitrary, but she comes to everyone. You must be ready to meet her.

How can you prepare yourself for meeting Fortune? The ancient Romans, so involved with the caprice of Fortuna, are the ones I turn to for guidance. My teacher Seneca, the wise old Stoic, whose essay on providence I have quoted before, offers a realistic appraisal. He notes that the most unfortunate among us are those who have never experienced bad luck. "Although all which exceeds limits may harm us," Seneca warns, "the most perilous is extreme good fortune; it agitates the brain, it summons false ideas in the mind, and it shrouds in murkiness the line between fact and fiction." In short, *too* good a fortune leads us to believe a host of untruthful things about the world and about ourselves.

In a startling metaphor, Seneca captures for me the contrast between those who suffer much ill fortune and those who seem to know only good luck: "Death from hunger eases gently by, while too full stomachs burst apart." The image underscores a reality easily missed when we are in our storms—ill fortune comes to all, sooner or later. But those who feast on their good luck are unprepared for sudden reversals and undone completely by them.

We, the lucky wet, are instructed by misfortune. I agree with my teacher that, "calamity is the occasion for virtue." It provides opportunity—and incentive—to improve our selves, if not our fortunes. In fact, as Seneca urges, "We should offer ourselves to Fortuna in order that, face-to-face with her, we may be hardened by her. A little at a time, she will make us equal to herself."

Step 7.

Get a Life!

I have a question for you. *Are you attaining success?*

This question is important to me—and I know it is to you, too. Look back over the first six steps. In the midst of a storm you took time to make sure to square the corners of the foundation of the Self. You began building conscientiously. Your growth has been inward, outward, and upward. With the expansion of your plan and your personal growth, you have become more capable than ever of identifying and managing obstacles. You are better at finding and seizing opportunities. You have reached a point where you can truly face forward with focus.

I am assuming your focus is on achieving greater success than you have ever known. So let's use that focus to really consider what success is. When we met and got started, I imagine your focus was limited to overcoming the storm. Whatever disappointment, setback, or failure got your attention also held your attention. Your initial interest was in finding some reason to hope that there can yet be more to life than wet weather.

You accepted my argument that your first need was to stay intact. Since that point you have been doing a great job at developing yourself. Whether you have realized it or not, what you have been proving is how able you are to be more successful being you! Whatever specific personal or professional dream you hold, it depends on self-development. In that respect, you may already have attained greater success than you imagined when we began this journey together.

Our English word 'success' is an adaptation from the Latin noun *successus*. Though that word could refer to 'an approach,' 'advancing uphill,' or 'an outcome,' our language adopted the last meaning. In English, success is what comes at the end; it is an outcome. Once, that was understood as referring to either good success, or bad success (like good fortune and ill fortune). Today, we tend to think of only a favorable outcome or result when we use the word.

There are some important things you can learn from this little dictionary exercise:

- If success is a result, then it can be treated as a *product*, the outcome of labor. This lends to you a measure of control over your success.

- Success can only be judged at the end of a sequence of steps. Until the outcome is known, judgment is presumptuous. You should avoid the extremes of cockiness and despair.

- When you judge something a success, it is because you have reached a favorable or desirable outcome. This is a relative, subjective appraisal. *You* decide if you have attained success.

So what is success for you? I hope it is realizing your potential as a person and finding satisfaction in that. I hope being all you can be is what you desire. I hope you understand that apart from that kind of success, anything else you accomplish will seem ultimately empty. A well-lived life is about being a self-realized individual.

Of course, that kind of success cannot be fully measured until we have reached the end of our life's journey, looked back, and reckoned that life has been as it was meant to be, with all its ups and downs. In the meantime, though, we can set for ourselves intermediate objectives with clearly defined steps. As we attain each step we can rightly judge it a success and reaching the next step we can call greater success. We can legitimately see ourselves as successful people as we build on one modest success after another.

Do you see now how successful you already are?

All Work and No Play . . .

And yet, I must still ask, *are you attaining success?*

I can tell you with each step how you are achieving success with that step. I can reassure you each step is leading to greater success. But I am not the judge who matters. You are. Success is in your hands. It is also in your mind.

I'm sure you remain wet enough from your storm to retain a few doubts about success. I know the tendency to focus on how much more you want, how far away your goal remains, and how things can always be better than they are. In short, I can imagine that despite your gains you remain restless, unsatisfied, and still in doubt about your future.

I have some advice for you.

Get a life.

Seriously.

Stop obsessing. The nature of loss, disappointment, failure and setback is a restriction of life. We narrow our horizons, sometimes so severely we end up staring at our navel. I have confessed how, in my storm, all I could see at first was the mud. I was tempted to wallow in it. My vision had narrowed to a single point in my experience.

All my energy went into overcoming the storm. But in my zeal, I forgot that between the drops of rain was the very air my life depended on. To put it more bluntly, I stopped paying attention to things that mattered more than my being wet. I neglected my health, my friends and family, the sources of joy still left to me. In my desire to bounce back and prove myself more successful, I was failing to live fully.

I had to be confronted with the question, *are you attaining success?* And I had to admit, 'no, I'm not.' Just finding satisfactory work and earning a living was not enough. If that was all I meant by success, then I was failing myself.

Let my experience be a warning. You will fail to see the forest if you concentrate on one or two trees. Even if you reach the tree you obsess over, it won't be enough. That great professional success you hunger for—the big income, the fancy toys to display your wealth, the envy of others—won't mean much against the gaping holes left from inattention to what life is really about.

Life is always in the living. *Things* are dead. Living is about experiencing, not acquiring. Life is love and suffering, not profit and loss. If personal development is measured solely by professional attainment, then living has been exchanged for a résumé. Life is reaching, stretching, and growing.

The problem remains that storms direct our attention down a narrow tunnel. We obsess. In the storm, life may seem to demand all work and no play. You may tell yourself you don't deserve a break, or fun, until you have dealt with the crisis at hand. You may tell yourself you must reach final, ultimate, and complete success before you are entitled to any reward.

The truth is very different. Living is its own reward. The wise Preacher of *Ecclesiastes* reminds us, "whoever is joined with all the living has hope, for a living dog is better than a dead lion." The lion may lay claim to the title 'king of beasts'—a distinguished *product* to be sure—but the dog possesses the *process* of living, and process trumps product. In the quest for success, don't forget the greatest success is living.

Pay attention to the basics. Get enough sleep every day. Eat regular and balanced meals. Exercise. You know the drill—are you doing it?

Living a healthy lifestyle has direct bearing on your ability to succeed in your specific objectives. A healthy lifestyle adds energy you can draw upon. But merely going through the mechanics, treating sleep, diet, and exercise like they are dots to be connected, can be a joyless affair. Life can be reduced to a packaged product, but that isn't living.

You must get a life so robust it crowds its energy into every cell of your body. Here are a dozen tips from my own education in the school of hard knocks:

- Look up and about. See life abounding around you.

- Call a friend and chat about nothing in particular.

- Find something funny to laugh about.

- Stop counting pennies for a time and start counting blessings.

- Take a walk with a loved one and hold hands.

- Sing a happy song.

- Visit someone you haven't seen in too long.

- Enjoy a meal sitting down, with conversation on the side.

- Buy yourself a present—just for being you.

- Go smell a flower.

- Read a book for pleasure.

- Play.

Here is a simple exercise for you during this week: each time you do one of the above, put a check mark and a date in front of it. Prove to yourself you have control enough of your life to do healthy things.

Never cheat yourself of a chance to live in the moment. By successfully living one moment at a time, you will eventually realize your entire life has been the success you always wanted.

Your Values, Your Life

Earlier, we saw how success is largely a matter of the mind. You determine how successful you are. Judging whether you have reached the success you want is a highly personal thing. Regardless of what others think, you will know inside yourself whether you are attaining success.

What determines the judgment you make?

Your estimation of your success follows from your values. If you conform closely to the values of our wider culture, you will judge yourself successful if you acquire wealth, a good standing among others, relative freedom from pressures and constraints, and happiness. The exact amount of how much of each of these things you need to feel successful will probably reflect your expectations from your upbringing, social circle, and estimation of your own capabilities. The advantage of this approach is that if you meet the cultural standards by which each is measured, you will probably feel successful. Certainly, those around you will see you in that way.

There are several disadvantages to this approach. First, you might meet the standards that win the applause of others and still not have met your own. Second, adopting the standards of others without consciously deciding for yourself that they are what are best for you can mean feeling hollow even though every indicator says you are a success. Third, the cultural standards set a bar that only a few can attain. Not everyone is going to acquire enough wealth, status, freedom and leisure to be successful by these measures. In tying yourself to them you may be needlessly setting yourself up for disappointment. Finally, these values may have little relation to the meaning of life. Many a 'successful' person by these standards has expressed great regret at life's end for not having focused on other values, particularly love.

So what are *your* values?

In order to more accurately measure your success, you need to spend time clarifying this matter. Your values are what you hold as most important. They are what bring you meaning. They are the basis of how you decide right and wrong. They define your character.

Try the following to clarify your values:

1. Spend a day letting the notion of values percolate in your mind.

2. Now, sit down and list what matters to you. I have provided space below to do this. (There is also extra space provided on page 68.)

    My Values

    ·

    ·

    ·

    ·

    ·

    ·

3. When you have finished, rank them. One way to determine their relative rank is to ask of any pair of them, which would you choose if you could have only one?

4. As you review your list, ask how each contributes to your personal plan for success.

5. Next, ask how each judges your plan. The higher the value, the more important the judgment it makes.

Are you measuring up to your own values? *Are you attaining success?*

Often, we place ourselves in a peculiar bind. We talk one set of values and live another. What we say matters most to us constitutes our 'espoused values.' Typically, they are things like family, God, and putting an end to world hunger. They are high and noble ideals. What we actually do reflects our 'practiced values.' Our actions prove what really matters to us—at least so far as how we choose to spend our time. Typically, these are things like personal appearance, leisure, and material property. In other words, we spend much of our time grooming ourselves before a mirror, taking time for television, and shopping.

A value conflict arises when we see the discrepancy between our espoused and practiced values. We might say we put our family first, but tying up the bathroom while we get our hair just right says our own appearance matters more. Put in that manner, we may feel guilty and shallow. The best way to resolve such conflicts is to narrow the distance between the espoused and practiced values. In short, by stopping our hypocrisy and living what we preach, we will feel better.

Go back to your list of values. Do the following:

1. Rank the list again, this time by how much time and energy you really devote to each. This will reveal your practiced values.

2. If you know you are showing some values in practice that you did not include in your list before, add them.

3. Decide whether this rank reflects what you really want.

4. Now, place a check beside those of your values that are mostly espoused and not practiced.

5. Consider whether they are important enough to warrant more practice of them. If so, write down suggestions of things you can do to put them into practice more.

6. Go back through the whole list and put everything in the order of how you want it. There is space provided at the end of this point for you to do so. For values that are more espoused than practiced, you now have ideas as to how to increase their practice. For ones more practiced than espoused you can decide whether to increase your verbal support of them or decrease your practice of them.

My Values (Reconsidered)

-
-
-
-

.

.

You have now both clarified your values and worked on resolving any value conflicts.

Working with your values is important. You become clearer about who you are. You learn more about what you see as constituting success in life. You stay focused on what matters. As you achieve success, you find meaning it.

But be wary. Values are sharp as swords. Your values can ennoble you—or afflict you. Having too few values can mean too little engagement with life and meaning. Having too many values can mean granting too much importance to too many things. Also, the more values you hold, and the more tenaciously you hold them, the greater the likelihood of trouble with others. Clashing values generate interpersonal conflicts.

Values may seem more trouble than they are worth. Yet we need them to feel fully alive. By giving us a sense that something matters they become fixed points on the compass we use to navigate life. In keeping us on course they also provide a way to gauge our progress. As we make them our own, they also make us their own. Ultimately, we reflect in our living what we judge life to be about.

So why have I waited so long to bring such matters up? You may wonder why this step was not the first. But consider. Could you have heard me tell you, 'Get a life!' when we first met? In the tumult of the storm, when the rain was heaviest, were you willing to pause and play? Could you have set your espoused values over against your practiced ones?

This step is right where it belongs. When you completed the sixth step, you were facing forward with focus. Now you see what you were ready to focus on. In overcoming your storm, keep your sense that the warmth and light of life is in daily living what matters most.

Are you attaining success?

Extra Writing Space for Exercises

Step 8.

Help Others

Here is another question to ponder: *Can you succeed alone?*

Writing is a lonely occupation. I sit in front of a computer screen for hours each day. No one tells me what to say or how to say it. In the splendid isolation of my office I easily can imagine that my work—and its success—is entirely mine. But that self-conceit defies the facts.

My success depends on connections with many others. First, I depend on the support of friends and family. They give me the space to write and the encouragement to endure the uncertainties of the business. Next, I rely on the support of a publishing house, especially the editors who work with me, to take my work and shape it into the form you hold in your hands. I depend on booksellers to place it on their shelves. Perhaps most of all, I rely on forging a connection with you. Without you my work remains unfulfilled.

Obviously, even such an individualistic endeavor as writing requires connections with many other people. We are social beings by nature. Our success as persons and as professionals occurs fully within the context of human relationships. In fact, we eagerly desire the approval of others as we seek to develop our own persons and the work that becomes an extension and reflection of our identity. We want those we care about to share in the glory of our success and to enjoy with us the rewards of our labor.

I know you know these things. Perhaps you are also aware of the paradox that life's storms can thrust you into. The storm says 'every man for himself!' You may feel abandoned or betrayed. Connections were broken and your sense of trust violated. Withdrawal from others serves as a reflexive self-defense against further wounds. Feeling wet is a lonely and isolating experience.

Thus, while we realize intellectually that we need others, our gut still reels from the role some have played in putting us out into the fury of the storm. Perhaps no other step to greater success may feel more counterintuitive than reaching out a hand when we feel as though we have just been pushed to the ground. Yet the rewards that come with connecting to others are immeasurable. Through others lies the vital path to connecting with tremendous success.

Acquire a Perspective

If life is a journey, then people are both our fellow travelers and signposts along the way. Most of those we meet are in encounters so brief we have little sense of their own journey. To us they are just signposts. But we would do well to pay close attention to their messages. Even causal inspection of what they say may change the direction of our travel.

When things seemed worst for me, I hardly knew which way to turn. Every direction looked equally dark. But then I realized I was only staring at my own navel. No wonder I was mired! In order to get off the side of the road and on my way again, I had to look for signposts.

What I lacked was perspective. My inability to see past my present circumstances and myself meant I could not acquire a broader context in which to interpret my experience. Like someone trying to walk on one leg, I lacked balance. The wonder wasn't that I kept falling into the mud. The wonder was that I had to do it so many times before I started looking up and around for help!

The turning point came one day when a friend inquired as to how I was faring. After offering my usual full round of 'woe is me,' our talk turned to mutual acquaintances. The conversation quickly settled on a lady with whom I had worked for about eight years. Despite intense pressures at her place of work, with complete lack of support from her supervisors, she managed not only to do her job with distinction, but also to rally the morale of all those around her. I had great respect for this woman and I wondered how she was doing. My friend brought me current on this lady's fortunes.

Her mother was gravely ill and would soon die. Her husband suffered from a cruel, debilitating disease. Her grown daughter was receiving experimental treatment for a baffling cancer. Since she had herself experienced cancer, she knew firsthand the uncertainties and fears her daughter was facing. Her house showed signs of structural damage requiring immediate attention. At work and at home, this woman had significant stressors.

Next to her, my storm was a lonely rain cloud and hers a hurricane. Yet while I moped in the mud, she strode against the whirlwind. I had never heard her complain about her lot in life. She faithfully attended to her mother. She was her husband's lifeline to the world and his primary caregiver. She was in constant touch with her daughter and made the several hours drive to be with her whenever she could. At work, despite unfair accusations by those who called themselves her friends, she hid her tears, put on a brave smile, and carried on.

She inspired me. I mean that literally. My attention drawn to her, I was made to lift my face, draw in a deep breath, and reconsider my world. If what had happened to me was unfair, this lady's travails were criminal. She was a good person in every sense, with never an unkind word about anyone else.

Thinking of her inflated my sagging spirit with wonder, respect, resolve, and appreciation.

If *she* could cope, so could *I*.

In a sense, she permitted me to stand upon her shoulders and gain a height from which a new perspective on misfortune and success was possible. For this lady is a great success. In fact, I know no one I consider more successful at the things that matter most in life. Though I would rescue her from all the suffering that surrounds her if I could, she rescued me from my myopia. Simply by being who she is, she lent to me a measure of strength and helped me regain my balance. *And she never knew it.*

Suddenly, the scales fell from my eyes. I was on the road again and I saw signposts all about me. Each sign was a person, and each person helped me keep my balance as I tried to reenter the world. Let me give you a few examples. I saw:

- a partner, who had huddled with me in the dark, holding out a candle by which I might see my way;

- my father, concern etched in his face and voice, always ready to believe the best of me and to say so;

- a friend, recently emerged from a storm of his own, eager to reciprocate the support I had offered him;

- a casual acquaintance, eyes wide open, who saw my pain one day and offered time to listen;

- a stranger who, from the wellsprings of her own humanity, eased my way with a simple act of goodness;

- a woman wallowing in self-pity who served as a mirror to my own soul; and,

- a man, who once I regarded as a friend, paying a heavy price for the sacrifice of his conscience in acquiescing to the evil set upon me.

These signs, both pleasant and unpleasant, provided me with a context for perspective.

Broaden Your World

Every sign, in its own manner, helps you get moving again and moving in the direction that is right for you. Some are cautionary in their lessons; others are inspiring. If only for a moment, as you read each sign you catch a glimpse of the traveler. They remind you that every life tells a story. Every person is a sign with a message for you to read.

Are you taking the time to read what is right in front of you?

Take a moment right now to look around yourself. Answer these questions as honestly as you can:

1. Who are the folk providing the signs I need to see right now?

2. What are those signs saying?

3. How will they change my journey?

Every sign—every person—you connect to right now becomes a post you can cling to for balance.

This simple exercise may help you gain perspective. Take a little time right now to answer each question from above in the space below. Come back to this list during the week and add more answers.

My Answers to 3 Important Questions

Who are the folk providing the signs I need to see right now?

-
-
-
-
-

What are those signs saying?

-
-
-
-
-

How will they change my journey?

-
-
-
-
-

Something marvelous can happen when you look to others. You gain the possibility of seeing life through eyes other than your own. Although you may not experience the world exactly like others do, you can join their experience. Through the power of the human imagination, drawing upon your own experiences, you can put yourself in another's shoes and let them carry you to places you might not otherwise ever see.

Although our steps together have concentrated on your personal development to achieve greater growth and success than you have ever known, you have never walked alone. I have been at your side—one human link in the chain that joins you to all humanity. Hopefully, your link to my experiences is broadening your world. Although all of us have a penchant for insisting on learning our lessons the hard way, the wise profit from the experiences of others. Just as there is no need to reinvent the wheel, there is no need to learn everything in life the hard way. Instead, broaden your experience by connecting to the hard won lessons of others.

Let's see how broad your world is right now. Take a sheet of paper, or use the space I have provided here, and complete the following as best you can:

1. Name the person you know whose experience seems most similar to your own. In one sentence, state as precisely as you can how your experiences match up.

Person:

Sentence:

2. Name the person you know whose fortunes in life seem most opposite your own. Set up two columns. In the left column list the ways this person's fortune is so different. In the right column list any ways this person's experiences and your own match up.

Person:

How different   *How similar*

3. Name the person whose success most looks like the success you hope for yourself. Match as many points between your own life and this person's experiences as you can.

Person:

My Life   *His/Her Experiences*

4. Name the person you know who has the most interesting life. List the things that make that life so interesting.

Person:

What makes this person's life so interesting is . . .

-
-
-
-
-

Although you have only named four people, what you see in them reflects much of your perspective. The first person shows your ability to see how others are like you and how you see yourself in them. The second displays how you contrast yourself with others and whether you have much ability to find points in common with even people who seem so completely different in their life situations. The third indicates the kind of person you might want to be like and a potential mentor. The fourth points to the kind of experiences you find intriguing, whether you want to have such experiences yourself or not. Those experiences offer potential avenues of insight into your own dreams and fears.

Collectively, these four people represent the breadth of your connection to the human experience. If you had trouble thinking of people to complete this exercise, you might want to consider taking more time to see others and understand them. If your trouble was in picking one particular name from the many that suggested themselves, then your world may be especially rich in connections. That means you have an abundant wealth of experiences others have won that you may be able to profit from. Regardless of how easy or difficult you found doing this, you can practice broadening your world and widening your perspective by paying attention to the messages offered by other lives.

Connect with Others in Service

We all owe much to those around us. From our parents who brought us into the world to our loved ones who escort our bodies to the grave, our lives are joined to others. While it can be all too easy to blame others when misfortune strikes, we often find it hard to credit those who have helped us to succeed. Thus far in this chapter you have been continuing to accumulate your debt to others. You have looked to others as signs along your way and sought help in their experiences. Now it is time to begin repaying your debts.

Let's begin with the following important exercise:

1. Take some time right now to reflect on the debts you owe. List the people in your life who have been instrumental in getting you to where you are. You may wish to use two columns—one for those who have helped you and the other for those who have opposed you. (We are known as much by our foes as by our friends.)

People I am indebted to:

-
-
-
-

2. For the list of those who have helped you, place a check beside each person you know you have taken time to thank. Consider if it is time to thank them once again, this time by some tangible demonstration.

3. For those you have not thanked, now is the time. Do it for each one as you feel most comfortable. You can use the phone, send a card or note, or visit. Be specific in what you are thanking them for.

4. For your list of foes something else is in order. It would be presumptuous of me to suggest forgiveness. If that seems suitable to you, so be it. But I do recommend considering a larger picture. As Joseph in the Bible realized, sometimes what others have meant as evil actually works to the good. Can you see a way in which the evil others has done to you has been transformed by you and your allies into something positive? Redirect your bitterness and anger toward them as gratitude and appreciation for yourself and those who have stood with you to redeem something of value from the evil you suffered. List a few of the ways you have wrung lemonade from the lemons in your life:

-
-
-
-
-
-

This exercise is meant to continue helping you with your perspective and sense of balance. It also prepares you for what comes next.

Those who do best in life are those who relate well with others. You can never get too much practice developing your social skills. The forming, building, and maintaining of relationships provides you a rich context in which your personal growth will bear full fruit. As you look toward greater success than before, connecting with others in service affords a path to reenter the world in a productive, meaningful fashion. It reverses the myopia induced by the storm and gives you farsighted vision to build a better world as you pursue a brighter future.

I challenge you to find ways to extend your network of connections with others through service. I understand you may feel like you have little to offer. Your resources may seem so depleted that the idea of giving appears ridiculous.

What I want you to grasp is that *everything you have accomplished to this point has made you ready for this*. In tending to your own care you have made yourself a person who has much to offer others simply by being yourself. Genuine service to others is always an expression of who you are. With the careful attention you have given to yourself, you can now trust your ability to extend a helping hand.

Allow me to suggest some ways in which you can find a freeing self-expression in service:

- Say "thank you" to someone who has helped you by doing him or her a quiet, unasked for service.

- Seize a few unexpected opportunities to help strangers, such as assisting an elderly person, carrying groceries for a mother trying to manage small children, or giving up your seat to a pregnant woman. The deed need not be large to be greatly appreciated. And it will enlarge you.

- Consider volunteering for some group to which you already belong. Churches, synagogues, mosques and temples seem to always have worthwhile things for volunteers to do, both short term and long term. Or perhaps you are connected already to a fraternal organization, a club, or an organization like the scouts. These groups also offer ways to help others.

- Mentor someone less experienced than yourself in an endeavor you both find meaningful.

- Choose an activity you enjoy (perhaps a sport or making something), and volunteer assisting others who enjoy the same thing. This can be done on your own or through an organization.

Of course, you know yourself best. Find—or create—personally meaningful and distinctive ways to reveal the person you are and are becoming.

Bit by bit, you can reestablish, and extend, a valuable network. You will stand at the center as a person rich in humanity, willing and able to enrich others. All of us are known by our behavior—by what we do. *You* will be known as a person of compassion and service. Others will witness your growth through the crucible of your own suffering. They will see you becoming a person of ever increasing success as a human being. And you will be the kind of person anyone would prefer to deal with professionally, no matter what your occupation or business is.

Finally, there remains a peculiar debt I would ask you to not overlook. The experience of suffering links us to the community of sufferers. That bond carries an obligation to render the aid you so desperately needed—and received. I would especially urge you to turn your attention to someone else in a storm. Helping others who hurt puts your own pain in a new light. Everyone experiences misfortune. Assisting another person through her or his storm will help you to not feel so chilled by the rain on your own head. More importantly, it will accomplish the power of love, which joins us with others in a process of mutual growth.

Step 9.

Implement Your Own "I" Strategy

I am impressed. You have made it through eight challenging steps. The first six prepared you to more fully consider the nature of success—the seventh step—and to be ready to attain more success than you ever have. The eighth step placed success in the context of social reality. Our success depends in part on others, is shared with others, and can benefit others. The success of personal growth completes itself in the love of an extended hand.

So what else is there?

You still need an effective daily strategy for coping with problems as they come—and perhaps before they arise. Once this storm has passed, another will come. Life is a rhythm of sunny and stormy days. You have chosen in this storm to seize the chance to become a better person. You have set your feet on the path to greater success. Now you can take all you have mastered and use it in a strategic plan.

This plan I call the "I" strategy. An important theme of my approach proclaims that proper attention to your personal development will yield dividends in character growth, professional achievement, and relationship building. It can seem selfish to concentrate on yourself. Yet, as with most things, there is an appropriate way to devote attention to yourself, and an inappropriate way. I do not advocate being like Narcissus, who preferred to contemplate his own image above all other things. Recall how I chided myself for navel-gazing and a myopia that kept me from seeing beyond myself.

Proper self-attention is teleological. The end, purpose and design it entails centers in a development that advantages yourself, others, and the world. The philosophy is this: by attending to my own needs and growth, I can prove myself capable of meeting my needs and developing my potential. As I do so, I become healthier. As I become healthier, I stand in a better position to help others. As I help others, the world becomes a better place. From my abundance comes fruit to nourish the earth.

Likewise, having a strategy to handle problems advantages everyone. You feel and function better, relational problems are dealt with responsibly so that others feel and function better, and the world is a little nicer place for everyone. Keeping your own "I" front and center serves as a win-win strategy. You win; so do others. The most enjoyable relationships reflect this reality. So do the most satisfying professional relationships. When you are realizing your potential as a person, you are simultaneously expressing your growth through your professional dealings and relationships. No wonder other people want to be near you!

An effective "I" strategy draws an exuberant 'Look what I can do!' from your own lips—and approval from others. You need never be embarrassed by your desire to realize your potential. You are not cheating anyone else. In fact, by our very nature as social beings, our full potential inevitably means becoming more successful in relationships. Think of it in this way: you have a relationship to yourself and to others. Paying proper attention to your own person is a gateway to proper attention to others.

In this step we are going to rework and integrate the previous eight steps. We are going to formulate a life strategy for self-development on a day-by-day basis. This strategic plan incorporates all you have done so far. It formalizes those things into a simple model that utilizes five basic tactics. By practicing these tactics you will be continuing to implement all you have learned.

Identify Problems

First, each day identify problems. You can't fix what's broken until you know what it is. As your skill grows in recognizing problems, you will find you can anticipate some problems *before* they happen. This is called 'learning from experience' for a very good reason! The ability to stop a potential problem before it becomes an actual problem will save you a world of grief. It is the equivalent of practicing preventive medicine instead of waiting until you are sick to see a doctor.

Your preventive plan won't work unless it is a daily regimen. I recommend two formal periods of problem identification each day. In addition, I recommend a habit of informal problem review as needed during the day. Here are some specific recommendations for a daily schedule:

My Daily Schedule for Problem-Working

1. Start first thing in the morning while preparing for the day. Do a mental review of all plans for the upcoming day. Prioritize. This may be pursued while doing such automatic tasks as getting dressed or eating breakfast. It need not take long, but it should be thorough in specifying each problem area intended to be addressed today.

2. Occasionally during the day, while actually working on a problem, pause to reassess both the nature of the problem and the desired outcome. How is it going? This is particularly important to do whenever

feeling frustrated. Frustration is a learned feeling, one that comes when progress toward a goal is blocked. When frustrated, use that feeling as a signal to mentally reappraise what is happening right now. Perhaps the immediate problem is a misidentification of the ultimate problem, or the desired goal. Frustration might signal trying to fix the wrong thing or having an unrealistic goal. Be realistic as well as persistent.

3. Make the last thing done at night before bed a review of what was done during the day *and* some brief planning for tomorrow. Focus on the process used during the day and don't forget to acknowledge (and feel god over) the progress made, however little or much. In preparing for tomorrow, limit a 'to-do' list to no more than 5 specific problems anticipated for addressing tomorrow. Commit to progress on at least 3 of these, in order of priority as decided in the next morning's review.

The purpose of the daily schedule is to make you a problem-solver every day. Don't think of this as resigning yourself to dealing with hassles every day for the rest of your life—though that is probably true!—but see it as making it so much a part of how you deal with life that today's problems soon become just another set of challenges. (And if you need additional help in managing life's everyday stresses, pick up my little book *Twelve Magic Wands: The Art of Meeting Life's Challenges*.)

Let's try this process out, starting at the last step. Below, list 5 specific problems you intend to address tomorrow. Remember, you don't have to solve them. You don't even have to make progress on all of them. But you do have to make progress—however small—on three of them. So, first list the problems:

*   Problem 1:

*   Problem 2:

*   Problem 3:

*   Problem 4:

*   Problem 5:

As you go through the day tomorrow, start with step one. Prioritize by putting the problems listed above in order according to their importance to you, or their immediacy. Be careful not to get in the habit of letting the merely urgent crowd out the truly important.

- 1st priority:

- 2nd priority:

Notice you only need to prioritize one or two problems.

Take time as the day unfolds to jot down any thoughts on each problem as you are working on it. These might include feelings, too. Note both good and bad. Brainstorm. The main point is to demonstrate you are working on the problem.

- Notes on 1st priority:

- Notes on 2nd priority:

- Notes on other problem(s):

Now, at the end of the day, review. If you only made a little progress on one problem, that is still better than no progress on any problems—so celebrate all your successes rather than dwelling on any failures. However, do note what might have kept you from meeting your goal of making progress on at least three problems. In other words, if you don't meet your goal, ask yourself why, think it over, and make better plans for tomorrow. Here is space for reviewing:

- Review on 1ˢᵗ priority:

- Review on 2ⁿᵈ priority:

- Review on other problem(s):

Be sure to complete the process by identifying problems to be worked on tomorrow. It's all right if they are the same ones. Some problems are very resistant and some may even be permanent. It isn't that we *have* problems that matters; it's what we *do* with them that matters. If you have done this exercise once, you can certainly do it again. (But you'll have to supply your own paper!)

Of course, you may be unsure exactly what kinds of problems you should be giving attention to, especially if you are like me and some days seem to have so many problems no list can be long enough. You will want to know exactly what it is you are reviewing and identifying.

Problem identification in the sense I mean requires attention to several matters. It is directly tied to the success we have been discussing—your growth in pursuit of realizing your potential in all spheres of your life. You should not be surprised, then, at the following areas needing daily attention:

1. your character; this matter needs each day to receive priority attention. What character issues are limiting you right now? How will you become a better person today?

2. your relationships; these display to others your character development. With whom are you having problems currently? What area in which relationship can you improve today?

3. your profession—meaning what you profess about yourself in the things you do. This may or may not be your actual job (it might be an avocation you find more personally expressive of who you are). How are your actions showing—or hiding—the real you?

4. your specific external difficulties; the hassles of the day such as unexpected bills, car problems, or other unpleasantness that cannot be simply ignored. Which of these are truly important? Which are urgent, needing immediate attention? How will you solve the problem so that it promotes your self-growth?

On any given day, you may not identify a problem in one or more of these areas. Not all of life is circumscribed with difficulties, no matter what the storms of life suggest. Still, each area should be reviewed for problems, or potential ones, every day. Prompt identification and swift response can nip problems in the bud and keep you on track in your pursuit of success.

Ultimately, though, which problems you identify and select to work on is far less important than that you are actually working as a problem-solver. Trust me—it is far better to be a problem-solver than troublemaker.

Improvise Solutions

Having identified problems, you need solutions. However, you will miss the mark if you narrow your understanding of 'solutions' to 'products.' The most significant solutions are actually processes that day in and day out keep you moving forward. What matters is *progress*. Just as Rome was not built in day, neither was the empire dismantled in one. Handling problems is an ongoing work that keeps building your self, your future, and your greater success.

At the heart of an effective process for problem-solving is the art of improvisation. Life seldom yields to a by-the-numbers approach. Looking for pat answers is a self-limiting option. The most brilliant strategy planned before a battle must give way to in-the-moment tactical adjustments if it is to succeed. Everything you have learned to this point has helped you become a flexible, growing individual with abundant resources to meet the challenges you face.

What is an effective improvisation? The art of improvising in problem-solving has these elements:

- preparation;

- creativity;

- relevance; and,

- spontaneity.

Though improvisation is in-the-moment, it does not rise from nothingness. Every present moment draws on elements from the past. Your job is to make sure the elements you draw on in the present are appropriate to the need at hand.

Preparation reflects your having ready at hand the resources to solve the problem. This avoids the panic coming from being caught unprepared and unaware. Preparation lends you confidence. You know you can cope. You aren't afraid to depart from old answers that never worked well. You are proactive in making changes to advantage yourself.

Creativity is born of the freedom to try new things. Because you aren't bound by old solutions you can brainstorm alternatives and then experiment. Since creativity, like life, possesses energy and movement, you don't sweat it too much when early efforts prove less wonderful than you had hoped. You know that creating also involves testing, revising, and trying again. You find it exciting to see how your skills at solving problems expands.

Relevance comes from being free of irrational fears and insecurities so that you can focus on the problem. Without distractions you see the problem clearly and direct your energy squarely at it. Relevance guides your creativity. It shortens the time problems require. It encourages the liberty of spontaneity.

Spontaneity is the culminating and defining element of improvisation. It is not a knee jerk response to make a problem go away, or to resolve it at once no matter how poorly. Instead, it is the energy made possible by the other four elements. When problems surface, so too does the immediate power to begin handling them. Because you can trust yourself, especially your preparation and creativity, you expect that your process of coping will be relevant. At any point in the process of handling the problem you anticipate a sudden breakthrough in the way you see the problem, respond to it, or manage it.

If you review each of these elements in light of the first eight steps of this book, I think you will see how practical everything you have been learning is to solving problems. Even as you weather the storm that started you on this journey, you develop skills to manage future storms. Although no plan can keep you free of an occasional dousing, the resulting rain merely nourishes you growing soul. You may never enjoy problems, but you need not ever fear them. In perfecting the art of improvising solutions, you show exactly the kind of person you are truth becoming: an individual who is continually growing and adapting in a self-directed quest for greater success.

Imagine Success

The 'realism' of pessimism is too often a self-fulfilled prophecy. If you expect things to go wrong, you may be unconsciously sabotaging your own efforts. While some research suggests that pessimism has its place, that place is not in the midst of your efforts to solve problems. Instead, imagine your success. Do everything with the expectation that it can succeed. Visualize proving your competence in meeting the need at hand.

Imagining success actually is very realistic. The energy it summons is positive—and well earned because of the personal development you have pursued. Rooted in an accurate appraisal of the problem at hand, you immediately know success is not merely possible, but inevitable. Because you are unafraid of the process, reckoning the time it takes as well spent, you know you can hold a vision and shape the progressive steps to reach it. All this work is practical.

Here are some ideas as to how to utilize this skill:

- Start by cutting the problem down to size. In the first blush of trouble, many of us have a tendency to blow the problem out of all proportion. Rob it of this emotional power by seeing it more objectively.

- Leap ahead through the power of your imagination to the outcome you desire. Don't confuse the outcome with success. By now you have learned success is more about process than product. But the outcome is important as a guide to your steps and as a culminating reward to your efforts.

- Visualize a series of separate, discrete steps to move you closer to the outcome you envision.

- Take each step in turn, using the improvisational art you are mastering. Expect twists and turns. Proactively make changes in your steps and vision.

- Accept reversals as opportunities. By keeping your eyes fixed on where you are going you will be less troubled by the occasional pothole in the road.

Now let's try this out with an actual problem. Select any one you like and go through the above steps in the space below:

1. *Cut the problem down to size*—write as exactly as possible, without exaggeration, the *facts* about this problem:

-

-

-

-

-

-

2. *List a step-by-step process to solve the problem:*

-

-

-

-

-

-

Remember, it is always easier to reach a goal that you can see—even if only in the imagination. When you engage your imagination to visualize success you minimize setbacks and keep your focus. Don't forget the other points, such as expecting twists and turns. Your plan has no guarantee of success, but you are pretty much guaranteed failure without one!

Imitate Role Models

Your fourth tactic is to imitate role models. This serves some important purposes. First, it helps keep your eyes off the muddy ground and away from your own navel. It encourages you to see the signposts offered by other people. It engages you in the world. Second, it utilizes an important resource—the wisdom and experience of fellow travelers. Third, it offers a way to see in action effective problem-solving. Fourth, it provides a potential channel for soliciting feedback as you attempt the same thing. Finally, it helps you learn in a way that you can eventually use to instruct others.

Albert Bandura and other psychologists term this kind of behavior 'observational learning.' We all use it. For example, watch children and see how many ways they copy the adults around them. This kind of learning, Bandura says, requires four processes:

- attention to the model;

- remembering what has been observed;

- imitation of the behavior; and,

- a motivation for imitation.

Let's put those processes into action.

Look around for people you admire and figure out why (attention). Study them until you have clearly in mind what they do that you want to copy (remembering). Emulate their tactics when faced with similar situations to the one you are in (imitation). Draw on something to energize your action—a desire to be like the person, a hope to have similar outcomes, or some other internal or external factor (motivation). Become like the people you admire and soon you will be distinctively successful in your own unique way.

Let's try it. Select one person you admire. It does not have to be someone you know personally, but it does have to be someone you can observe for a time.

1. Observe the person. Take notes of the behavior you desire to imitate. Write some ideas down here:

   •

   •

   •

2. Think about what makes this person's behavior so successful. What exactly do they do that is different from what you do? Write some of your conclusions down here:

   •

   •

   •

3. Put together your thoughts from steps 1 and 2 with the goal of creating an action sequence you can visualize and then try out. Write the steps of this action sequence in order here:

   •

   •

   •

   •

   •

When you are comfortable you have this sequence firmly in mind, can see it in your mind's eye, and feel ready to give it a try, then go out and put it into practice. Don't expect perfection—practice makes perfect, and you've just started. Keep at it and in time you will be doing what your model does, but in your own distinctive way. You can repeat this process again and again, building yourself more and more into someone others will want to imitate.

Impact Your World Positively

The fifth tactic is to positively impact your world. Most of us, most of the time, contribute our woes to the world's huge pile of troubles. We count ourselves casualties. We impact the world in a negative way, adding our problems to everyone else's. We use our problems positively when we publicly address them and present workable solutions.

As I see it, you can be one of three kinds of people: a victim, a survivor, or a savior. A victim suffers without redemption. A survivor experiences redemption. A savior extends a helping hand to other victims so that they can become survivors. You can change the world one person at a time—starting with yourself.

Aim at nothing less. *Make a difference.* Turn what you have learned into a better life for yourself and others. Try these things:

- Share your story. Talk not only about the storm, but about your success in surviving it.

- Teach what works. You can do this by becoming a model others will want to imitate and by finding ways to concretely set down successful steps for others to follow (through teaching a workshop, a class, or writing about your experience and learning).

Implement your "I" strategy, using these five tactics, today and for the rest of your days on this good earth.

Additional Writing Space for Exercises

Step 10.

Just Do It!

Look how far you have come!

For a moment, cast a glance with me back along the path we have traveled. We met in a storm. Now, it should not matter quite as much whether any raindrops remain. The clouds have begun to break up. Your patience and labor have brought you to where you can see patches of sunshine in clear skies.

Despite the negative circumstances in which you began your journey, you mustered the courage to take to the road. You affirmed yourself for solid reasons—and so squared a sound foundation. You soberly assessed yourself and realized how much you possess to build upon. Indeed, you discovered that the three essential keys to create the new knowledge and skills you desire are right at hand. You committed to using them to expand yourself. As you did these things you found it easier to embrace opportunities, which provide you new avenues of growth. No wonder, at the halfway point, you were well prepared to face forward with renewed focus. You had become capable of taking the next step—reconsidering and clarifying the true nature of success. You saw how it isn't a mere product, but a process of living. You pondered your values. Having completed such impressive progress, you honored your development by honoring others. You recognized your debt to others, your connection to them, and your obligation to help them. Then you summed up your labors by individualizing a personal strategy for ongoing identification and solving of new problems.

Now you have reached the final step.

I say without hesitation that it represents a great challenge. That challenge can be summed up in three words:

Just do it.

As a counselor and teacher, I have accompanied many people for stretches of their life journey. Some of these folk have enjoyed tremendous insight into their lives. They readily grasp what their problems are and the steps required to advance. And yet . . . after all is said and done, more is generally said than done.

To achieve the greater success you desire requires action. I am well pleased at the work you have put in to this point. Every exercise you completed offered to yourself, to me, and to others concrete proof of your seriousness about developing who you are and what you can accomplish. Yet, I know how hard it is to sustain effort. I understand how weary you become. I remember how often I have wanted to just lie down, to quit the struggle, to concede defeat.

The *desire* for greater success requires little energy; the *accomplishment* of such success requires sustaining great effort. However, there is good news. First, reaching your dream does not require perfection. You are an unfinished work and will remain so. All living things are unfinished. You need not beat up on yourself. Success lies in the striving and progress toward self-realization in your character, profession, and relationships.

Second, experiencing greater success is principally self-defined. Success is relative. By using your own potential as your measure, you can continually enjoy successes along the way to the full attainment of your dream. Free of a product orientation, you can genuinely taste the fruits of your ongoing labors. You don't have to wait to enjoy success.

Third, the effort required for greater success is self-renewing. Thankfully, a dividend of spending energy is accruing strength. Just as fatiguing exercise builds physical endurance, so striving for greater success liberates the power to press on toward yet more success. Because your success flows from you—and reflects you—the more you give, the more you get. Everything you have done so far, and all you will continue to do, represents a sound investment in yourself.

Let's return to the utility of a short alphabet to sum up the component parts of this last step out of the storm and into the full sun. Let's call this alphabet the ABCs of success: *act, build, complete.* These are the three capstone terms that enclose everything else. We might have begun here, but the first nine steps are all encompassed in this alphabet. Without them, this final step would seem hopelessly vague. Now, you can invest in these three words the wealth of what you have learned and practiced.

Act

Insight is wonderful. But without application, insight remains unfulfilled. All the knowledge in the world about what you need to do won't mean a thing unless you do it. So what prevents so many of us from acting? Why are we our own worst enemy?

There isn't any one reason that fits everybody. When I get bogged down and fail to act, generally it is because I am depressed. I can't see the point in trying; everything seems meaningless. My energy drains out. I sit in the mud.

What holds *you* back?

Think about the last time you did not do what you thought you needed to do. What reason did you give to yourself? Is that reason one you find yourself commonly using? Or do you have a set of reasons to defend yourself?

Periodically along the way, we have discussed the importance of self-talk. The language we speak to ourselves inside our own head largely defines our experience. No matter what is going on outside us, what we say about it inside ourselves makes a decisive difference. In order to succeed we need to master an internal language that advantages us rather than hinders us.

You have already learned how to identify and eliminate excuses (back in step five). Take time to review that material. Now consider these other common excuses for not acting. Note, too, the rational response you can offer to each.

- *Excuse:* "It isn't my fault. So-and-so is stopping me." *Rational Reply:* People can pose obstacles. But when Romeo wanted to meet Juliet, there were no walls too high, too wide, or too strong to prevent him. I can find my way over, around, or through this obstacle.

- *Excuse:* "I don't know how." *Rational Reply:* If I don't know how to do something, I can learn. So my progress will be marked first by my effort to learn, and then by my effort to apply that learning.

- *Excuse:* "It's too hard. I can't do it." *Rational Reply:* Many things are hard. Sometimes things are too hard simply because they are too large. Breaking down the task into smaller, manageable parts is something I can do. Besides, even if it turns out that I fail in my effort, I won't really know until I try.

- *Excuse:* "I'm not ready yet." *Rational Reply:* If not now, when? If not me, who? The bottom line here is that readiness and acting are my responsibility. If I'm not ready, I can get ready—and I can start right now.

- *Excuse:* "Why bother? It seems like a lot of work and it probably won't make much difference anyway." *Rational Reply:* There are no guarantees as to the outcome and product of my effort. But there won't be any outcome or product if I don't try. More importantly, I judge my success by my progress, which does make a difference.

All the skills you have learned can be brought to bear on overcoming your own resistance. In acting, the key element is *motivation*. What a crucial element that is! If I had a fail-proof method for motivating people, I would be the most famous and the wealthiest person in the world. In fact, those who prove most successful at motivation tend to be the most famous and wealthy among us. You cannot overestimate its importance.

While identifying and eliminating excuses to act helps, the central problem of motivation remains. In psychology, the study of motivation is a major topic.

There are many theories about motivation and no one theory has captured the field. The truth is, motivation has proven an elusive reality. Probably many factors come into play, with different people responding in various ways to certain ones more than others.

What motivates *you?*

Some of us are moved most by external factors. These include threats of punishment or promises of reward. Others move themselves mainly by internal factors. These include strong beliefs and desires. Add to these things the necessity of meeting our physical and emotional needs. Soon you see how complex motivation is for all of us.

Yet each of us is moved by some factors more than others. I am consumed by a lifelong compulsion to write. I don't write so much because I want to as because I have to—something inside me drives me. When I don't write, I don't function well as a person. None of that makes me a better writer (product), but it does keep me developing (process).

Once more I ask: what motivates you? Your actions will become more reliable as you identify these sources and intentionally draw upon them. For example, if you are motivated by a belief about yourself that you are the author of your own destiny, then you can use that belief to challenge yourself to keep moving. So take the time to carefully identify your personal motivational factors. Write here what motivates you:

Build

You doubtless noticed that in speaking of acting, I did not tell you *what* to do. Nor did I tell you *how* to do it. I focused on the *why*—the motivation needed. Without it, you won't act often or well. What you do, and how, is highly individualistic and situational. With the skills you have learned you can select the 'what' and the 'how' you need.

In building, the key is *step-by-step progression*. Greater success is achieved most often by one foot ahead of the other up a long climb. Don't expect someone to come swooping down from on high and lifting you to the summit. That would be looking for rescue, which you are perfectly capable of doing for yourself. Remember that tremendous satisfaction resides in the climb. After all, once your reach the summit, no matter how great the view, the only options are either down, or on to another, higher peak.

It may help motivate you to remember the stakes involved. You are intending nothing less than the progressive unfolding and realization of all your potential. This is not a sprint, but a marathon. As you develop yourself, your potential actually grows. You will never completely catch up to it, but you can push yourself well beyond what you presently envision yourself to be capable of. By taking one step at a time and focusing on each sequential step, you will attain realizable results—the products of success—while moving to, and then beyond, your original dream. How exciting it is to know that you are capable of more than you yet dream, and that you will exceed what you now imagine—if only you keep putting one foot in front of the other.

Don't worry about stumbles. I have adopted the philosophy that if I am going to fall while walking, at least I want to be leaning in the right direction when I go down. That way, even my failure is building my eventual success. You can do the same thing. You have already learned how to turn storms into opportunities and use rain for growth. You are the soil that life will water, if you have the courage to expose yourself and pursue your dreams. And you are brave.

In building success—an ongoing process—you will want to establish clear indicators to measure your progress. Here are a few building tips:

- Use your dreams to foster a vision you can sketch into a plan. This is a process of putting what you imagine into tangible form. The result is a planning guide. Be sure the planning guide is sequential in nature.

- Use quality materials. In self-development that means taking your time to do each step fully and correctly. Find the best knowledge, develop the best skills, and pursue the highest dream. Devote the best part of each day to your building.

- Focus on process. Product will take care of itself if you have a dependable process. Concentrate on doing everything the right way—honoring your values, developing your character, and enhancing your relationships.

- Take time to mark your progress by seeing how far you have come. This is itself a significant reward. You should take pleasure in it. Renew yourself with the satisfaction of work well done, replenish your energy, and move forward with confidence.

If you overreach on occasion, don't beat yourself up. Instead, interpret it as a sign of your eagerness, ambition, and belief in yourself. Learn from the error. Then start out again. Life encourages us by offering chance after chance after chance.

Complete

Achieving greater success need never end. Why would you want it to do so? Glory leads to glory. As you reach one objective another reveals itself. You need never be bored!

So why talk of completion? Completing is also a process, one in which effort is sustained through the accomplishment of an objective in order to head for the next one. The goal is always progress and development.

Completing means sustaining your motivational energy through all the building steps to reach a particular point. After all, you are not walking aimlessly. You are striding from point to point. Just as when traveling across the country you measure the trip by the places you hope to reach for refueling and resting, so in pursuing success you identify and travel to specific points. But when you reach each point you understand it is just a way station. The final destination remains in front of you.

The difference between building and completing, both of which are processes, rests in the nature of the pauses. In building, each pause separates the steps along the way. In completing, the pause identifies the attainment of a specific marker event. For example, if one objective is to learn a new computer skill, such as developing a web-page, then each lesson you take to reach this end serves as a step, with natural pauses in-between. You pause to note your accomplishment, consolidate your gain, and then you resume walking. When the skill is attained so that a web-page results, then you have completed the objective. The success is a marker event. The process has yielded results along the way that culminate in a particular outcome you envisioned from the start.

However, the building of the skill to make a webpage was itself merely one step in a larger plan. Your success in it is encouraging. Yet more work needs to be done. The objective is not the goal, just a marker showing your progress toward the goal. Your ultimate goal remains forever out of reach—to be all you can be.

The importance of completing is similar to following through on a motion in sports. A baseball pitcher, for example, continues his motion even after releasing the pitch. So does a basketball player after attempting a shot, a bowler after letting the ball go, and a tennis player after striking the ball. In each case, the motion is a natural part of all that preceded it. It also puts the player into position for the next move, whether fielding the ball, grabbing a rebound, picking up a spare, or returning an opponent's volley. You need to see completing as a process that serves as a transition between one thing well done and another waiting to be done equally well.

These ABCs—acting, building, and completing—name a style of life built upon all our steps. Now that you have taken this journey with me, we can sum up everything we have discussed quite simply. We can make this summary knowing how much is held in each part. If you are to 'just do it' in life, then . . .

1. Find a way to make yourself move.

2. Move one step at a time.

3. Keep moving from success to still greater success.

You *can* do it.

Conclusion.

Soaking in the Sun

After the rain, the sun shines brighter.

Really. The storm will pass, if it has not already. Regardless of where the storm is, you are in a better place. Even if you still feel damp, you should also be feeling the sun on your head. In my mind's eye, I see you having grown to a stature where your head now pokes through the clouds to the clear sky above.

The sun shines brighter because the water in the air makes it so. You may have to squint after becoming accustomed to the darkness. You may shield your eyes and wonder if anything so beautiful can be real. Trust the sun. Storms, with their wind and rain, are not the only realities in life.

So, as we stand together before the light of brighter and better days, it is almost time to say goodbye. But if you can be patient with me a little while longer, I would like to linger with you. Although we have completed the steps, there remain some personal words I would like to offer. These are things I reserve for my friends.

You might be wondering where the steps in this book came from and how well I do following them. Many of the things we talked about may have had the ring of familiarity. In part, that familiar tone comes from you and I sharing time in the same school of hard knocks. Indeed, anyone who has gone through a trying time has a sense of what we have shared. Although I may say things a little differently than you do, our common experience of suffering lends us a voice we recognize in one another.

Like you, I was wise enough to seek help wherever I could find it. My education, training, and professional experiences reside in the disciplines of psychology and religion. I have profited from both fields. Perhaps you recognized some of the concepts or suggestions because you have seen something similar elsewhere. Wherever I have borrowed directly from someone, as with Albert Bandura's ideas on observational learning, I have acknowledged it. However, many ideas have become so widely spread and commonly known that no one particular person has any real claim on them. What I have done is to find my own voice so that the expression of an idea truly reflects my thinking along with those wiser than myself. In this manner I have practiced imitating my models.

You will greatly honor me if you find things from our time together that you put into your own voice and share with others. I trust you will find creative ways to shape the raw substance of these pages into exactly fitting pieces for your own needs. Yet I deeply adhere to the premise that research and learning are not completed until they are offered to others. I had to share my journey and what I learned. I hope you feel the same pressure to share yours. In that way we will be joined on another journey, as fellow teachers and—perhaps—fellow healers.

This has been a small book—a short journey. As you move beyond me, I hope you will consider sharing with me the ways in which you advance beyond me. Perhaps you will want to share it with me in a letter. Maybe you will write an article. You may even have a book in you!

But before we leave, let's sit together in the sun a little longer. I have talked off and on about my experience of the storm. I have not spoken directly about my time in the sun. Yet there are lessons there as well. In the little time left to us, let me offer you some of what can be learned from days in the sun.

Enjoying the Warm Glow of Success

Perhaps I will sound unbelievable when I tell you that what I most want in life is to be a good person—a *mensch*. For me that means living honorably and peaceably. It requires honesty and compassion. Though I am by nature a person who craves solitude and thrives on silence, I am compelled by my notion of goodness to endure the chaos and tumult of the world in order to try to make a difference for others. I make no claim that my contribution is either majestic or enduring. But I strive to make it a reflection of myself and to bring to it the best I can muster in the moment.

If you measure success by wealth or fame, then you will have to look else-where. Money has never been much of a motivational source, even though I generally need more of it than I have! Many people have regarded me as an un-derachiever because of the places I have chosen to work and the salaries I have accepted. By cultural standards, I am just another minion, a part of the masses, nobody special.

Except, that I matter to myself. My spouse genuinely loves me—and likes me to boot. We share lives intertwined without being entangled. I know love and can only regret never being able to give it in the measure I receive. I am rich in friends. Their company warms me. These people are tangible measures to me of my success. They ennoble me.

You are entitled to define your own success and measure it how you will. Like most of us, you will probably do it in several areas. Throughout our time together we have spoken of character, relationships, and profession. In the sunlight all three look different than in the darkness of the storm. Their inner essence may remain substantially the same, but the degree of light causes us to see them differently. Use the light of this time in the sun to look afresh at all these things.

In emerging from my storm, I felt a renewed appreciation for my connections with others. The storm cost me some connections—and that hurts. Yet it strengthened others. In the sunlight I now see that some of the relationships I lost I am better off without. The people in them were only using me and had little compunction in discarding me. I prefer to relate to fellow travelers who are in this journey for the duration. Those people I see more clearly than ever.

I also hope I have learned better to stay in the moment. I envy my spouse, who does this exceptionally well. I remain a work in progress. I tend to watch vigilantly for clouds on the horizon and to forget to feel the warmth of the sun on my back. Still, the sun is teaching me to appreciate its waxing and waning, to see the cycles of life, and to permit myself moments to close my eyes and simply enjoy the sensations of *being*.

One Eye on the Clouds

I promised you at the start to be honest. I will now confess the painful truth that I can be slow to learn important lessons. Whether by temperament, or experience, or both, I remain plagued by certain disadvantageous characteristics. I am high strung, prone to anxiety and depression, and easily given to pessimism. In the sunshine, these traits are inconvenient but tolerable. In storms they make my life much worse than the amount of wind and rain justifies. So I am trying to use the periods of sunshine to make progress with each trait.

You perhaps noticed the unrelenting optimism of this book. The tone is meant as much for my ears as yours. I won't lie—I need to hear these things as much as anyone. I know that learning is consolidated through repetition. I fully intend to keep hammering all these points home to myself, rain or shine.

I will also keep one eye on the sky. By practicing these steps, you can do the same. Neither you nor I need be caught unaware. If it should pass that we are, practicing in the sunshine makes more likely managing in the rain. I know neither of us wants any more storms.

Yet life requires rain to nourish the soil of the soul. The storms have their place, however unpleasant they are. Whether we prefer the wisdom of Seneca or that of the Bible, both concur that testing refines us. I don't know whether I am a pupil in a cosmic classroom where misfortune signifies the teacher's keen interest in me. I do know that I disappoint myself when I let the fury of the storm diminish my humanity. I covet for myself the success that keeps me fully human—in the best sense of the word—whether in storm or sun.

Light and Darkness

The world's religions make abundant use of the imagery of light and darkness. Here is a picture we all understand. Our experience is not unmixed. We all want light and warmth; we all pass through cold and darkness. Just as every day fades into night, we can endure the darkness knowing the sun will rise again.

You have weathered the storm before, and you can handle whatever comes your way next. Still, it is easier for me to say that for you than for myself. The prospect of coming storms disturbs me. I harbor secret doubts about myself. But I am using the sun to expose those doubts and confront them now. I am preparing for the inevitable by the attentive work I do now.

Success remains a process. In retrospect, I see how my storm propelled me in the direction I really wanted to go. That does not make the evil done to me any less evil—and I believe one day we shall all answer for our deeds—but it shows how evil can be redeemed. Should evil come my way again—and it seems likely—I have the experience of knowing that good can and does eventually triumph.

As I grow older, I don't find darkness any more pleasant. I do, though, see better its value. As I look around me, writing in the late afternoon as the shadows lengthen, I realize that not even light and darkness are absolutely separated. They exist side by side. There were rays of light in the darkness of the storm. There are shadows in the light of day.

My task—and yours—becomes living in the duality of life. No matter what success we attain, it will never be unmixed. There will forever be shadows, degrees of disappointment and loss. They color our journey, and add dimension to our life experience. Let us learn to make the shadows catch the sun's rays more brilliantly. The beauty may take our breath away.

Finally, allow me to say how grateful I am you have trusted me with your company during this period in your life. Please remember my address. I'm not going anywhere. The next time you want to visit an old friend and ally, please drop by. Every time we talk we both have a chance to grow.

Additional Writing Space

I hope you will fill these last pages with your own notes and ideas.

Printed in the United States
111412LV00001B/162/A

9 780615 156323